THE POWER OF EXPOSURE: LESSONS OF SUCCESS FROM HIGHLY EFFECTIVE MENTORS

THE POWER OF EXPOSURE:

LESSONS OF SUCCESS FROM HIGHLY EFFECTIVE MENTORS

DAN M. DE NOSE

MANUSCRIPTS
PRESS

THE POWER OF EXPOSURE:

Lessons of Success from Highly Effective Mentors

ISBN   979-8-88926-074-5   *Hardcover*

979-8-88926-073-8   *Paperback*

979-8-88926-072-1   *Ebook*

To my forever love, Devonne; our children, Danae, Jayla, and Jeremiah; my parents Rosmond and Marcely; my sisters, Erline, Karen, and Barbara; my brother Leopold; and in loving memory of my brother Osborn—you were taken too soon, and you are greatly missed...

And to Wendy, Jim, Nate, and Jeremy, whom I've been blessed to have as my second family.

To every mentor who stood by me on my journey. You know who you are! When I felt like giving up, you encouraged and supported me in more than one way.

I thank God for you all.

Contents

Foreword

In *The Power of Exposure: Lessons of Success from Highly Effective Mentors*, author Dan De Nose offers readers a welcomed opportunity for inspiration and direction for mentorship in our challenged and polarized world. With a unique talent for storytelling and well-honed listening and research skills, De Nose draws from his personal narrative to chart a hopeful, accessible course for mentors and mentees alike. In so doing, he contributes a great deal to the literature as he opens an important conversation and advocacy for exposure mentorship.

De Nose's personal journey—from Newark, New Jersey, to Geneva, New York, to public service with then-Mayor Cory Booker, graduate school, corporate exposure, and education— is ample life experience for this dynamic young nonprofit leader to reflect at this stage of his career. De Nose provides a theoretical construct of exposure mentorship and offers a call to arms for colleges to collaborate and for high schools to partner with the workforce. He draws on his experiences for real-life guidance of networking (and his eight steps), public speaking, and branding with practical tips to achieve one's goals.

What distinguishes this book is its candid, vulnerable, and honest tone. While he is the son of a preacher, De Nose is never preachy. He opens up about his self-doubts and feelings of imposter syndrome and does not shy away from the important and interconnected issues of race, code-switching, and DEI.

A gifted storyteller, De Nose details his own observed experiences in compelling ways that allow the reader to feel like you are in the room. In turn, you are rooting for the individuals he writes about; you want Jeremiah, Elycia, and Elissa to succeed. And you are grateful for his parents, Wendy and Jim, Mr. H, Mr. Gerry, and Cory Booker, and their impact on his life.

De Nose urges his readers to "consider your journey as a collection of diverse puzzle pieces." It is one of many observations that one mines in his work. With his impressive nonprofit, Leaders of the 21st Century, Dan De Nose has put in motion his aspirations for our world and the potential of every human. Blessed with hard-working immigrant parents who inspired and motivated him to make a difference, he has honored them and walked the walk of service and community building.

For me personally, I was honored to be among Dan's mentors when he was an undergraduate at Hobart and William Smith Colleges, and I am grateful for his friendship. He is a blessing in my life. In reading this book, I also learned a great deal from his observations, provocations, and recommendations. Indeed, this mentor became the *mentee.*

Mark D. Gearan

Geneva, New York
January 30, 2024

Introduction

Everyone thinks mentorship is when someone shares their knowledge, skills, and experience with another person to help them progress in life. This mentor-mentee relationship usually involves a more senior individual to the more junior individual. Typically, these relationships are forged through pairings based on similar interests, possibly within a certain career field. The ability of a mentor to build a strong relationship allows the mentee to position themselves for a career they are interested in. It is an important aspect of professional development and helps the mentees navigate this process. A successful mentor-mentee relationship requires effort and commitment from both parties.

I am writing this book to advocate for change in the way businesses, colleges, government, and educational programs prepare the future workforce. This information is intended for those entering the workforce and those in the position to mentor and create change within their industry. A better system is necessary to equip the current and new workforce with proper guidance and understanding on how to navigate the twenty-first century in a global economy. If we do this right, the integrity of the economic security that impacts our country's families will strengthen the economy as a whole.

I have witnessed some of the brightest and most talented youth miss out on opportunities simply for not knowing the right people or never receiving proper training on becoming a professional. If they have never met a professional, how can they emulate one? This challenge is even more pronounced for immigrants or first-generation college students who may not have had the opportunity to witness and learn from professionals in their respective fields. This disparity highlights the importance of addressing these gaps in mentorship and training to empower aspiring individuals from diverse backgrounds to thrive in their professional journeys.

We owe it to our children and their children to create a world where diversity, equity, and inclusion exist to provide them access for upward mobility.

I'm going to further this concept of mentoring as an effective model that can be replicated in schools, businesses, and organizations through the process of exposure mentorship, through which the mentor and mentee can foster a successful relationship beyond their current role.

Do you remember when you were a kid and you dreamed about what you wanted to be when you grew up? I am that same kid who, despite the passage of time, still clings to dreams with the same fervor.

From an early age, I harbored a vision of leaving a lasting impact on the lives of young people, offering them an experience akin to what I had in my youth. It dawned on me, even in my early years, I had been singled out for a purpose greater than myself.

It was the day after my college graduation when destiny decided to paint a headline across the front page that read, "Change the World." There was a black-and-white snapshot of me crossing the graduation stage. In one hand, I held my hard-earned college diploma, while the other was raised in a triumphant fist. Adorned with a Haiti flag and representing Hobart College, my beaming smile reflected the realization of a dream that once only existed in the realm of imagination. It was a moment that brought me one step closer to my heart's desire of changing the world. That day is etched in my memory, a beacon of accomplishment.

As the pages of time turned, the luster of that dream began to fade. Many years have passed since that iconic moment. The truth is, I was one decision away from giving up on my dream until I heard the words, "Don't be discouraged; stay encouraged." I was never given a handbook on how to build a nonprofit, but the mentor who shared these words with me had. He is now serving as my executive leadership mentor providing me with exposure, insight, resources, and connections.

I believe when a mentee can see themselves represented in their mentors' positions, it provides them with a tangible example of what they can achieve. Role models play a crucial role in inspiring and motivating individuals from underrepresented backgrounds to pursue their goals and aspirations. When you are given exposure mentorship, mentees can develop the confidence, knowledge, and connections necessary to navigate their chosen paths. They can see firsthand their dreams and aspirations are attainable, and they are not limited by their circumstances.

But what is exposure mentorship?

A twenty-six-year-old named Aura works as an optometrist for Warby Parker. Prior to this career, she worked in the office for an ophthalmologist. Surprisingly, she had no interest in being an optometrist, but because she had been exposed to this work, she discovered she had a passion and interest for this career. Soon after, the ophthalmologist became her mentor and motivated her. Now she works for a great company who provided her the opportunity to go back to school and receive her education in this field.

When I asked if she would be where she is today in this field if not for her mentor, her response was filled with conviction: "No." She went further and said, "I only wish I was exposed to this field when I was in high school. I would have been further ahead in my career."

Exposure mentorship is the power shared from mentor to mentee. It is a form of mentorship or guidance relationship in which one person, often more experienced or knowledgeable in a particular field, provides another person with opportunities to gain exposure and experience in that field. The mentor, in this case, acts as a guide and facilitator, helping the mentee access and navigate opportunities that will enhance their knowledge, skills, and network. This type of mentorship can be particularly valuable for individuals looking to break into a new field, advance their careers, or expand their professional networks.

On Saturday, October 15, we held our second session of the 2022–23 school year for our fellows in Leaders of the 21st Century (LOT21C). We have been providing leadership and professional development to high school students in the city of Newark for seven years. We deliver a highly tailored leadership, career readiness, and professional skills curriculum that also pairs students with a professional mentor who provides insight and exposure to their career.

That morning felt different because the day's schedule included two career exposure mentors. The focus for that day's workshop was foundational principles of leadership and effective communication. Our speakers, Joy and Mike, were no strangers to our program: Joy had been around for five of the six years we were operational, and Mike served as a junior program facilitator one year. Joy presented on time management, and Mike presented on interviewing skills.

How does one manage their time if they cannot manage themselves? I thought as Joy began her presentation.

As with many years before, she gave a dynamic presentation. Our students were engaged, asking questions, applying what they learned from her in real time. I had seen the presentation many times over, yet a student asked a question I'd never pondered: "Why aren't we being taught this in school?"

This was where my quest began. Aura and my student both made me realize that if not for the organization inviting Joy to come in to present on the topic, this student—a junior in high school—might not have ever been exposed to the fundamental skills of how to manage one's time. Many of our schools follow a traditional model of education that places the teacher in a role where they are seen as the enforcer of rules and knowledge.

According to Dr. Jennifer N. Calico, this model relies on testing, textbooks, and students mastering the material. The other form of education is a progressive education model that places students in the center of the education model that allows critical thinking, problem solving, and most importantly inspires students to be lifelong learners. Dr. Calico, who has a doctorate in educational leadership and curriculum and instruction believes this model allows the teacher to be seen as a facilitator of knowledge.

Both models have the potential to guide you toward a successful life. However, it's important to note that specific professional skills are crucial for the transition from college to a career that are not covered by either of these models for aspiring students.

Aura and my student inspired me to take a deeper look into our current education system, as well as our college-to-career pipeline for minorities, and its relationship with mentorship and its impact on diversity, equity, and inclusion (DEI).

THE STATE OF THE UNION

The United States Treasury released an article titled "Racial Differences in Economic Security: The Racial Wealth Gap," wherein researchers at the Federal Reserve Bank of St. Louis found the median white family had $184,000 in wealth in 2019, compared to just thirty-eight thousand and twenty-three thousand dollars for the median Hispanic and Black families, respectively.[1] Moreover, their analysis shows the median wealth gap between white and Black families has hardly changed over the last twenty years.

The top 10 percent of earners held 66.6 percent of all wealth in the United States as of the third quarter of 2023. In contrast, only 2.6 percent of the total wealth was held by the bottom 50 percent of earners. Contrary to popular belief, the United States is not always a place where perseverance, hard work, or a college degree will result in success. In 2021, 9.3 percent of American families earned less than fifteen thousand dollars per year.[2]

The concept of "the more you learn, the more you earn" generally holds true in terms of statistical trends. Higher levels of education and skill acquisition often lead to better job prospects and higher earning potential. However, it is important to acknowledge that an "opportunity divide" exists in the US, particularly affecting minorities, which lessens the access to good jobs and career pathways.

The National Center for Education Statistics states the college enrollment in 2021, between the ages of eighteen to twenty-four years old, was 38 percent for white Americans and 37 percent for Black Americans. Despite the 1 percent difference with college enrollment between the two groups, jobless rates were higher than the national rate for African Americans with 8.6 percent compared to jobless rate for whites being 4.7 percent.[3]

Minorities—including individuals who may not have the opportunity to go to college or access other forms of advanced education—often face barriers limiting their ability to secure well-paying jobs. This can be attributed to various factors such as systemic inequalities, discrimination, limited access to quality education, and socioeconomic disparities. As a result, they find themselves on one side of the opportunity divide, struggling to access conventional job pathways and facing limited career prospects.

On the other side, employers also bear the impact of the opportunity divide. Many employers, especially in the middle-skill job market, find it challenging to fill positions with qualified candidates. This scarcity of skilled workers can hinder the growth and productivity of businesses, impeding their ability to compete on a global scale. The opportunity divide not only affects individuals but also has direct implications for corporate America's future as a globally competitive superpower.

MY CHANGE OF COURSE

During my undergraduate years, I had the privilege to be elected as a student on the Board of Trustees for Hobart and William Smith Colleges. At the time, I was unaware of the magnitude of this and how this experience would shape me into the professional I am today. I was made privy to confidential conversations. I watched how high-level executives for top companies interacted with one another and the confidence they exuded. I witnessed how to "move" in a room and how to be diplomatic when you agree to disagree. By comparing where I wanted to be in life, I realized I did not have the proper skills. It was also during this time I identified the need to build a team of mentors who served as bumpers to help me stay the course and gain employment post undergraduate.

It is very important to know that during this time in 2010, "The Great Recession" had officially ended in September.

Yet, according to Tony Cox from *Talk on The Nation*, unemployment remained high, foreclosures for many Americans continued, and President Obama called for a two-year pay freeze for federal workers. The total of unemployed people in December 2010 was over fourteen million based on the United States Bureau of Labor Statistics.[4] The economy was the subject of contentious debate. Families at dinner tables and students in classrooms were all discussing what the future would look like.

We were all living in an uncertain time; however, through a mentor, I was able to interview for a role as a "body aide" for the former Mayor of Newark, New Jersey Senator Cory A. Booker. It was also through a mentor that I was able to work in human resources for Prudential and become a community organizer around quality education. All my roles in life were afforded to me based on my relationships with my mentors. Yet I do not think I would have been prepared for these roles if not for my experience as a student, being surrounded by those who sat on the Board of Trustees. Despite the imposter syndrome I experienced for a moment during my undergraduate years, I felt I belonged in any room I was put in post undergraduate school because of my service on the Board of Trustees. I was exposed to many things, some of which you will find mentioned in this book.

I saw in my own life with my parents, who, unbeknownst to me, served as my first pair of exposure mentors. My mother and father, despite economic challenges, immersed me in the arts, summer programs, and travel. They provided me with a broader perspective and expanded my horizons. These experiences exposed me to different cultures, ideas, and possibilities, fostering an open mindset as well as a curiosity for trying despite the possibility of failing but more so on the experience itself. This exposure was transformative and the beginning of what shaped my ambition.

I grew up in an enriched Haitian culture where my parents' values were steeped in faith, love, and hard work. This laid a strong foundation for my personal and professional development. They allowed me to explore new opportunities and to make life-changing decisions. Witnessing their determination for their children to succeed in life instilled in me a strong work ethic I have carried throughout my career.

I always wonder as I daydreamed, the secret behind people's greatness. For the longest time, I believed it was solely due to their brilliance and extraordinary routines. Over the years, I immersed myself in countless books on self-improvement, professional development, leadership, and self-help. It wasn't until I reflected on my life experiences, acknowledging the privileges and opportunities I had access to, that my perspective began to shift.

Through my journey in the professional world, extensive research, and personal interviews, a revelation emerged—the often-overlooked factor that distinguishes between average and extraordinary is the presence of the right mentors. Yes, you read it correctly. The right mentor in your life has the power to transform you from average to extraordinary. Now, don't misunderstand me; nothing is inherently wrong with being average. The term itself suggests you and others like you share more similarities than differences.

However, envision this: having the right mentor is akin to placing an "X" on opposite sides of a loose-leaf paper and folding it in half. The mentor becomes the catalyst, drastically shortening your journey to your destination by sharing invaluable knowledge and wisdom derived from their best practices. Picture Yoda guiding Luke Skywalker, Professor X mentoring the X-Men, or Batman mentoring Robin. In each case, someone greater than the prodigy helped them unleash their full potential.

This book is an exploration of the transformative power of exposure mentorship. It's a guide to understanding how the right mentor can act as a beacon, propelling you toward new heights.

As we embark on this journey together, the focus of this book becomes abundantly clear. You will unravel the profound influence of mentorship, exploring its transformative impact on the mentee, the myriad doors of opportunity it opens, and the diverse forms this invaluable relationship can take. Throughout these pages, you'll discover practical tips on setting and achieving goals, an inspiration to reach new heights, and a reminder to embrace a continual willingness to learn from others while celebrating your own unique value.

As you reflect on the exposure mentorship that has silently shaped your life, I am compelled to share this reading experience will be nothing short of enlightening. The revelations within these chapters have unveiled layers of mentorship you will have never identified before. You will not only be enlightened but also deeply encouraged.

This book is tailored for individuals seeking successful navigation through mentor-to-mentee and mentee-to-mentor relationships. It's also crafted for those aspiring to advance their careers by delving into the lives of high-level leaders driving change within the DEI realm. If you're eager to unlock the secrets of effective mentorship, elevate your professional journey, and gain insights from influential leaders shaping the DEI landscape, this book is your roadmap to success.

So, dear reader, as you dive into the chapters that lie ahead, allow this book to be a guiding light on your path to personal and professional growth. Let it inspire you to recognize and appreciate the mentorship around you. After all, in the pages that follow, you may find not just words, but a catalyst for transformative change. Embrace this journey, and let the power of mentorship propel you toward your extraordinary potential.

Many who have achieved their dream roles benefited from the guidance of mentors or navigated the path through trial and error. This book is your gateway to an intergenerational perspective, featuring insights from college presidents, a *Forbes* 30 Under 30 recipient, nonprofit leaders, and individuals from the business world. The privilege of interviewing these exceptional mentors has convinced me of their remarkable contributions to creating diverse, equitable, and inclusive workforces, colleges, universities, and pipelines through exposure-driven mentorship.

Within the pages of this book, I share segments of their narratives along with some of their most successful career-related DEI strategies. These strategies have not only reshaped the way their organizations operate but also offer valuable lessons for anyone seeking to enhance their professional journey through effective mentorship. As you delve into the chapters ahead, may their stories inspire and guide you toward achieving your aspirations.

So, embark on this journey with me as we uncover the magic of mentorship and learn how it can be the key to unlocking your extraordinary potential. Happy reading.

CHAPTER 1

The Rejection That Changed Everything

As tears trickled down my cheeks, I was overwhelmed with gratitude. I looked into the mirror that morning and saw "Rutgers University Newark — School of Public Administration and Affairs" on my sweatshirt. This triggered memories of how I struggled academically as a student and how difficult my life was during my adolescent years. Here in the mirror stood a man who had received his master's degree and graduated summa cum laude—something I never thought possible.

Amid my reflections, I couldn't help but think of the pivotal role Wendy and Jim played in my life. At the tender age of eleven, they became my second parents. Realizing pursuing college meant leaving Geneva, New York, and my home city of Newark, New Jersey, where my family resided, I faced a difficult decision. It seemed unfair to part ways with Wendy and Jim after six years under their care, yet staying away from my mom and dad felt equally unjust. After visiting Niagara University, the decision became clear: I had to go to college.

The campus was beautiful, and the distance from both families would help me avoid this guilt of choosing one family over the other. The goal for leaving Newark was to increase my chances to graduate from high school and attend college. This was the reason so many caring adults invested in my growth. They saw something within me I did not at the time see.

"Wendy!" I said with a joyful melody. "I belong here. This is where I want to be."

Wendy, being the gentle-hearted mother she is, responded, "Great, all we have to do now is apply."

As we drove back home on I-90, all I could think about was how great a school Niagara University would be and how I would excel on this campus. I remember visualizing with my eyes closed living in the dorm and building myself into a productive student. I was certain I would be accepted—so much so this was my only choice.

Once I sent the application, I found Wendy in the kitchen preparing dinner and Jim outside cutting the grass. I waited for Jim to come back inside. With a proud smile, I told them Niagara was my only choice.

With a concerned frown, Wendy said, "Have you considered applying to a backup school? Just in case you do not get in, it would be good to apply to a second school."

To appease Wendy, I asked, "What other school do you think?"

With a nurturing tone, she said, "Hobart and William Smith Colleges."

I took a second to gather my thoughts so the tone in my response was not rude. "Wendy, if you think I should apply, then I will." Honestly, I said this only to make her feel good.

My heart beat against my chest like a herd of panicked horses in a wild stampede. It was nerves mixed with excitement and anxiousness. This was my first letter of acceptance, and it would be the only letter of acceptance I needed.

As I grabbed the letter, I caught a glimpse of Wendy's eyes, and I instantly knew something was wrong. I paid closer attention to the envelope and realized something peculiar. My friends from school had mentioned their envelope was as thick as a stack of quarters. I opened the letter with anticipation and read, "Congratulations." Were my eyes deceiving me? It continued, "Dear Dan De Nose, after carefully reviewing your application, we regret to inform you that…"

I couldn't read on. Disappointed was an understatement. I was crushed. Wendy leaned in and gave me a hug and reassured me everything would be all right.

Days after being rejected, I hoped and prayed Hobart and William Smith Colleges would accept me. The letter from them finally arrived, my stomach sunk. But when I opened it, it read differently: Hobart and William Smith Colleges admission decided to put me on the waitlist. I was upset, frustrated, and hopeless. The letter instructed me to write a letter of continued interest so the school would keep me on the waitlist.

I said to Wendy, "They don't want me, and I am not going to go to a place that does not want me."

Wendy tried to reason with me and show me the bigger picture, but my judgment was blurred due to my ego blocking my logic. In hindsight, Wendy's guidance was a good reflection on parenting and mentorship. Her experience as an educator provided me with great insight; however, as a teenager, I overlooked this reassurance. What other options did I have?

"I know," I said to myself. "I will join the military. Maybe this is what I was always meant to do."

I did not want to pick up the phone and call my family back in Newark—the people who had sacrificed and counted on me to go to college. My options were now limited, and I could not call my biological parents and let them know their son had failed them.

"The squeaky wheel gets the oil," Jim always said. I never thought I would have to apply this adage in real life, but I had no choice.

I knew I would have to find a miracle to get my name removed from the waitlist and to be enrolled as a first-year student.

I wrote letters and called the admissions office often to find out if they changed their mind to enroll me. Friends and people I considered family petitioned on my behalf, telling the school if they did not take me in it would be a great mistake. My mentor, Father Adams of St. Peter's Episcopal Church and Director of Lake Delaware Boys' Camp, and his wife Sue Adams, reached out to their peers and informed the school I would be a great asset to their prestigious institution. So, I did what any person with faith as small as a mustard seed would do: I prayed.

Another familiar day as a senior in high school—the hallway was filled with laughter and rushing footsteps to make it to class on time. You could overhear congratulations from friends letting each other know of the many colleges acceptances and scholarship money awarded to them.

"Dan," I heard through the crowd, "someone from Hobart and William Smith Colleges is here to meet with you in the counselor's office."

I thought this was a bad joke, but judging by the look on the guidance counselor's face, I could see he was being sincere. With nervous anticipation, I hurried over to the counselor's office with my head up high. My high school counselor mouthed some words of encouragement, but I could not decipher what he said. My focus was on other things anyway.

This could be my only shot to get into college, I thought. What words could I share to have them reconsider my entry? It is hard to explain, but I began to understand what Harriet Tubman said when she crossed the line: "There was such a glory over everything."[1] I felt a level of peace and determination as I got closer to the office door. When I entered the room, the admissions counselor offered me a seat.

After he introduced himself, he explained he was here to interview me. Once he finished his introduction, I said, "You have to take me into your school."

He responded, "Excuse me?"

"You must take me into your school," I said with conviction. "Here is the reason why!"

I do not know what came over me or why he allowed me to continue, but I told him my story from birth until that very moment in the office. I told him how during the delivery, my mother and I almost lost our lives. I told him how my family moved from Brooklyn to Newark for a safer environment, although Newark at that time was just as bad as any other urban city, if not worse. He sat with a blank face. He did not show any emotion. But that didn't stop me. I went further to explain how I had difficultly speaking as a kid and some of my first words were not until I was three years old. I explained how I went to a professional singing school, Newark Boys Chorus School, through which I traveled around the world, sang in Carnegie Hall, and on *Good Morning America.*

I told him about how I struggled in school as a boy and how I would get into fights, suspensions, and detentions. I told him how I attended a military-style summer camp called Lake Delaware Boys Camp. I said, "This is where the camp directors, Father Adams and his wife, proposed the opportunity for me to relocate to Geneva for a change of environment because they felt I was becoming a reflection of my environment." I told him how I moved from Newark to Geneva, a Black boy who took a leap of faith and now lived with a white family. He continued to just look at me, and I was not going to let him get a word in. As the great motivational speaker Les Brown would say, I was hungry![2]

When I exhausted all my words, the admission officer said, "I am going to return to my office and share my notes with my team. We will be in touch."

Once he stood up, I did as well and shook his hand, as gentlemen do. I said, "Thank you for making time to meet with me."

The first person I told about the meeting was Wendy. She and I were optimistic and had a good feeling. A couple of weeks later, I received a letter in the mail stating I was accepted into Hobart and William Smith Colleges. My unconventional approach paid off in a way that surpassed my wildest expectations. Faced with the uncertainty of admission, I took control of my destiny, and the result was a testament to the power of determination and the extraordinary impact of embracing one's own path.

FRESHMAN YEAR

My first year in college, I had no clue how to navigate the next four years of my life.

Confidence was something I never lacked on the surface, but deep down, I felt like an imposter in the classrooms and on campus. I leaned on my strengths to get through high school. My sense of humor would make the educators laugh. The charisma and charm would get me out of detention. The goal was to use my strengths and work on the areas I needed more support in as a teenager. Now that college was the next step, the jig was up; I would be exposed as a fraud, all of my weaknesses as a student out in the open. Academically, I was an average student. Based on the research I'd done, Hobart and William Smith was ranked among the top one hundred national liberal arts colleges by US News & World Report.[3]

I don't know how I will graduate in four years, I thought.

My mind created self-doubt, and personal incompetence creeped into my thoughts. *I don't belong here.* How could I, the same kid who struggled in middle school academically and was an average high school student, make out in this college? On campus, I saw some students from wealthy families driving my dream cars. I heard students speak to one another asking, "Where do you summer?"—a verse I understood was associated with those from the upper class. How could I possibly compete and succeed on this campus? I was not sure what I would do, but I had a laser focus on only two things: graduate in four years and become the best version of myself.

My friends were very supportive and we looked out for one another, but I knew something was missing. I needed an extra boost of knowledge and wisdom that could not be taught in a book but through someone else's experiences. I heard the quote, "Ask not what your country can do for you—ask what you can do for your country."[4] John F. Kennedy urged American citizens to participate in public service both locally and globally. The one phrase from his brief, fourteen-minute inaugural speech appealed to volunteerism. I realized mentorship is a form of public service through volunteering. It is connected directly to making our country better, and I needed someone who believe in his message as much as I did to mentor me.

Since campus was only a five-minute drive from my home in Geneva, I would take advantage of a home cooked meal.

I helped set the table while Jim and Wendy prepared the plates. We sat down, and Jim blessed the food. "Dear Lord, we thank you for the food we are going to receive and thank you for bringing Dan back home to join us for dinner." As Jim continued to pray, my mind drifted off to something I had to speak to Wendy and Jim about.

"Jim and Wendy," I said, "I have been thinking for some time about something, and I wanted to hear your thoughts."

Wendy responded, "Sure, what's been on your mind?"

Forks hit the plates as we ate our meal. I said, "I realized I need someone to really teach me how to become a better leader. I think I know who the person is who could help me." Jim and Wendy both took a moment to listen attentively as I took a sip of water. "I want to ask the president of my colleges, Mark Gearan, to be my mentor."

They exchanged looks, as if there was an inside joke I did not know about. Wendy said, "That's great news. Are you sure you want to ask him? He is extremely busy and has a lot on his plate."

Jim chimed in, "Yes, Dan. He may be too busy to take on the role."

Wendy and Jim knew his bio, which made them prepare me for the possibility of him saying no. It's a good thing I didn't understand the magnitude of his accomplishments, or I would've surely backed out of that idea. I simply thought, *Who could be the person to help me become the best version of myself?*

I was never told how to approach someone as your mentor. A class or book did not explain step by step how to formally ask. Due to my first formal mentor experience, I share with the kids I mentor within my organization the best way to go about asking for mentorship. If you feel a connection, simply invite the potential mentor out for coffee. During your coffee meeting, explain to them where you are along your journey as a leader and professional and that you are looking to learn from them.

It is important you both lay out expectations and a timeline on the relationship. What I discovered when seeking a mentor is how crucial it is to be sure the mentor is aligned with the direction you are heading in your life. They must be a fan of yours and committed to your success as much as you are.

The next day, I reached out to his assistant and asked if I could have a meeting with President Gearan to ask if he could be my mentor.

I could hear her smile through the phone when she responded, "I will set the meeting up for you."

FINAL LESSON

The journey in life requires courage to seek guidance in shaping your leadership journey. You will have moments of complexity as you navigate critical life junctures, battle imposter syndrome, and struggle to bridge the gap between perceived inadequacy and ambitious goals. But as my dad would say, "You are the master of your destiny."

Even on the toughest days, the right mentor is just an email or meeting away, ready to provide the guidance needed to overcome obstacles and continue on the path to success. They are your guiding light to advise you along the stormy sea with resilience, mentorship, and an unwavering belief that you have the power to shape your own destiny.

The important lesson is mentors and caring adults see potential in you often before you see it in yourself. From struggling academically in my adolescent years to graduating summa cum laude with a master's degree at Rutgers University Newark, the journey is a testament to resilience and the transformative power of education alongside great mentorship.

Having a clear goal in mind of what you want to accomplish truly sets the stage for your personal growth to thrive. The exploration of seeking mentorship by someone who shares similar values and goals will set you apart.

Overall, the major takeaway lessons revolve around resilience, the impact of mentors, and the transformative journey from adversity to personal and academic achievement. You are destined for greatness in every endeavor you pursue, so never lose faith in yourself! Right now, you're just one step away from turning your dreams into reality. Embrace the journey, believe in your potential, and watch as you transform your aspirations into triumphant achievements. Keep pushing forward because greatness is within your reach!

CHAPTER 2

Beyond Imposter Syndrome: Conquering Self-Doubt with Mentorship

In my first year as a college student, I did not have an understanding on how to do research prior to meeting a potential mentor. In hindsight, it was good at the time because, if I did my research, I would have been too nervous to go forward with seeking a mentor.

When I entered his office, President Mark Gearan greeted me with a handshake. I felt as if I had walked into the White House. There was a sense of prestige wrapped with a historical timeline that reflected a sense of leadership, service, honor, and humility. A Goldendoodle slept on the green-and-purple carpet that matched Hobart and William Smith Colleges' colors, alongside what looked to be a cherry oak presidential desk.

President Gearan ushered me in with a gentle, fatherly voice. "Come, please have a seat."

I tried to not get distracted, but it was hard not to notice all the pictures on the wall. In one, he was giving President Bill Clinton a high five. In another, he was walking with President Clinton along the West Wing,

A black-and-white photo showed Hillary Clinton and him facing one another with a big smile as if they won an election. Below was one in a beautiful black frame with handwritten words from Hillary Clinton. I looked at the photos of his family, his wife and daughters, graduation hoods hanging off the wall, African art, Peace Corps artifacts, and Madeline Albright, and a shelf filled with books. I was in awe.

I approached a colorful two-seater couch adorned with vertical stripes. A round, glossy coffee table between us, President Gearan sat across from me in a burgundy chair covered in gold stars. It reminded me of what our founding fathers might have had. It was majestic. Children's art was posted throughout his office that looked to be from his oldest daughter. As I continued to look around, I thought, *Who is this guy? Why does he have so many photos of the Clintons? Why would she personalize a photo for him?*

I snapped out of my trance, but my nerves kicked in. *Why are you here, Dan?* I reminded myself. *You have to shoot your shot*, I thought, which is a colloquialism term for, "You have to be brave and do something you're scared to do."

"President Gearan," I said with a hint of nervousness, "I know you are extremely busy and have a lot on your plate; however, I really want to learn how to become a better leader. As I was thinking of who could help me succeed to this end, I thought you would be the best person."

He looked at me through his glasses with his lips pursed in a smile.

I continued. "I wanted to know if you could mentor me."

Without hesitation or reflection, he said yes. "I don't know how we will do this, but I can share with you opportunities that come across my desk."

I said, "Thank you. That sounds great!"

During that time, I did my research on Gearan, and needless to say, I was impressed. President Gearan had a career largely in public service, either in government or higher education. Gearan had served in a variety of roles in American politics and government, including White House Communications Director, White House Deputy Chief of Staff, Vice Presidential Campaign Manager for Clinton and Gore's 1992 run, and Executive Director of the Democratic Governors Association.

In September 1995, President Bill Clinton appointed Gearan as the fourteenth director of the Peace Corps. There, he oversaw the expansion of the program into South Africa, Jordan, and Haiti. During his tenure, the Crisis Corps was created. It sent ex-Peace Corps volunteers to crisis areas for up to six months to provide assistance during emergencies. A cum laude graduate of Harvard College and Georgetown University Law Center, Gearan holds thirteen honorary degrees.

When I read all of this, I was flabbergasted and intrigued as to why he had agreed to mentor me. At the time, I had no clue what a mentor was. I simply knew a mentor was someone in a position to help you. Him saying yes was the beginning of my transformation into being the leader I am today. Although at the time I had no clue of the impact he would have on my life, let alone on the world, until I worked for him.

My first office job came during my sophomore year, working for President Gearan. He offered me the opportunity to come in during his assistant's lunch break to do administrative work. It was a couple of hours a week. On a regular workday, I would answer the phone and take messages until his assistant returned. On this particular day, people were coming in and out to meet with him. However, they were not entering through the same door a student or an employee would enter. This piqued my interest.

During one of our frequent meetings, President Gearan pulled me into his office for our routine check in. "Dan," he said with a warm smile, "there is a position on campus that I think would be a good fit for you."

I said, "What is it?"

He explained, "Student trustees are students representing the Hobart and William Smith student body who act as members of the colleges' board of trustees. As a group, members of the board of trustees make decisions affecting the everyday lives of the students. That means they work within the coordinate system. The board decides the policies the campus students must follow, and it also chose our new president. That means the student trustees play an important role in allowing students to have a voice."

I still had no idea what that all meant, but because he suggested it for me, he must have believed I was a good fit. I said enthusiastically, "I will do it."

"Well, you have to run for the position," he said.

Leaving the meeting, I felt encouraged and motivated about the possibility of being on the board. This would be my first taste of politics and participating in a college student-wide election.

The campaign turned out to be a battleground. It was a microcosm of real-world politics where I understood the importance of a grassroots approach of a campaign. I had weeks of sleepless nights, radio interview debates, T-shirt campaigns synchronized with the day of the week, and public interviews to spread my message to the campus: unify and serve all students. It was well executed, thanks to my campaign manager and classmate, Innis Baah. There was a recount and a runoff between me and another great candidate. We were told this was the first time this many students voted. We both knew only one could win. Nonetheless, if I was to lose to him, I knew it only reflected it was not meant to be for me. The school would have been in good hands if my opponent won.

Students had conversations throughout the campus about who was better qualified for the position. The anticipation of awaiting the election results was akin to a suspenseful journey. With each passing moment, my emotions oscillated between hope and apprehension. This agonizing discomfort continued for the days.

After the final recount, I was elected as a student trustee. This influenced and broadened my understanding of good leadership. This is the point at which exposure mentoring started to take shape.

By this point, I was beginning to understand what regular mentorship entailed, having worked with Mr. Gearan for a while. I had not known about "exposure mentorship" before. However, when I was invited to fundraising events to speak and raise money for the colleges, and when I networked with successful alumni, I learned how to navigate conversations. I also learned to connect people by listening to their interests. This enhanced my understanding the many levels when it comes to good leaders who are professionals versus great leaders who are professionals.

These were some of the valuable lessons I learned from being in the room and having lunches with board members. The memory that stands out the most during my time on the board was when one member seemed unlikely to mentor me. His profession was of no interest to me while I was a student; however, the time spent with him gave me a boost in confidence I still carry with me to this day. His name was Richard Wasserman.

Dr. Wasserman is board certified by the American Board of Allergy and Immunology and the American Board of Pediatrics. He received his medical degree from the Icahn School of Medicine at Mount Sinai/University of Texas Southwestern Medical Center and completed his Pediatrics Residency at Children's Hospital of Philadelphia.

One day, Dr. Wasserman gifted me a book called *Big Russ and Me: Father and Son: Lessons of Life* by Tim Russert. In one part of the story, Tim went for an interview and was not confident he was a good candidate for the job. While the other candidates waited to be interviewed outside in the hall, Tim Russert discovered they all came from Ivy League schools. Although Tim had attended a really good school, he felt he did not have the same chance as his peers. He entered the interview and told the hiring manager he was not a good fit for the role because the other guys were better.[1]

The hiring manager then said something that stuck with me. "What they know, you can learn. What you know, they can't learn."[2]

This imposter syndrome carried over from my first year to my sophomore year. Being in my junior year, the small waves of the feeling like I did not belong soon vanished. In many ways, this book from an unlikely mentor exposed me to a new way of thinking and shaped my perspective on how I viewed myself. I conquered the self-doubt associated with imposter syndrome and became more open to taking on challenges, pursuing opportunities, and embracing new experiences. The shifted mindset led me to being more optimistic and having an empowered outlook on my abilities and strengths.

During my senior year, an unexpected event cast a shadow over my college experience. President Gearan, grappling with the loss of his mother, was away in Massachusetts for her funeral. One late evening, as I found myself in the comfort of my on-campus house, my cell phone disrupted the quiet. The illuminated screen displayed the words, "President Gearan." Puzzled by the late hour, I hesitated before answering, assuming it was a misdialed call.

"Hi, Dan. How are you doing?" he greeted, unknowingly setting the stage for a conversation that would alter my perspective in an unforeseen positive way.

"I'm fine." But the truth was I was not fine. He returned and asked if I had time to come by his office.

When I arrived, his office lamp was on, but it was dimly lit. He offered me a seat, which I took, attempting not to show any vulnerability. I told him I was sorry to hear about the passing of his mother. He told me how much of an impact she had on his life. We shared a few more words about his mother, then the conversation shifted to me.

He said, "I was given word about an incident that happened while I was away, and I wanted to check on how you were handling all of this."

I was baffled. I thought to myself, *How is it that he is dealing with the passing of his mother yet called me to his office to see how I was doing?* I let my vulnerability shield down and poured out my overwhelming thoughts of frustration. He listened as a father would a child. Our conversation continued for nearly an hour. This taught me a valuable lesson. Mentorship often happens informally, in the quiet moments of removing the traditional hat of a mentor and connecting beyond the surface on a personal vulnerable sense. He exposed me to what true active listening looks like.

In that moment, I grasped that the role of president meant more to him than just a title; it was a life calling that extended beyond the traditional duty of leadership. It encompassed the profound responsibility of positively influencing the lives of his students for the betterment of the world.

When I met with him in the spring of 2023, thirteen years after that conversation, I wanted to figure out if he had a formula to his success. I always wondered what made President Gearan enter this specific field as a president of a college. Was it his upbringing? Here, an older white man wanted to mentor a young Black man, but why? What made him so special?

During this Zoom interview in the office of my home, I decided to pull back the layers. I asked what made him go into this field of work.

"It's sort of an opportunity," Gearan said. "I feel like doing my part to make a difference, whether that's in public service directly working for elected officials' administrations or in higher education. I think they are joined, at least in my own mind, by that centrality of what can you do to make a difference. People do it in all sorts of ways and in all sectors."

I nodded with excitement. I had this wonderful opportunity to receive gems to pass along to others to aid them along their path to success.

Mr. Gearan was not able to identify a name of an early mentor, but in reflection, he defined mentors as "people who just have an instinctive sense, clear sense or a declared sense, that they have your best interest in mind. They have your back, and they will do what they can to effectuate that." The earliest mentor was his mother and his family who provided enormous mentorship for him.

As I looked at the computer screen, I thought of an old childhood saying: "Your parents are your first teachers." Like many of us, we have modeled our behavior from what we witnessed from our parents, their work ethic, their empathy, and even their discipline. In other words, the first people who serves as mentors to many of us are our parents.

Growing up, I did not think of my parents as my mentors, but research would say otherwise. In her article, "Parents Can Be Mentors, Too!" Julie Link Roberts states that "mentors combine the roles of teacher, counselor, and coach as they work one on one or with a small group of young people. For purposes of this discussion, parents are mentors when they nurture interests, encourage and further the development of abilities and talents, and support a child as he or she endeavors to reach goals. They combine expertise with encouragement as they mentor a child or young person."[3]

I sat in my chair and said, "Wow. That's great," after I heard Mr. Gearan's definition.

I needed to know what advice or lessons he gained. I knew if I could receive the lessons he had learned through his mother and family, it would reinforce the lessons needed for those who would one day read this book.

He responded, "I think in the classic definition of mentor, I would say for me, initially, it's sort of just the power of observation. You can have just the opportunity—the privilege, really—to observe people. It sounds passive, and it doesn't sound substantive, but for me it's pretty powerful to observe styles you would emulate and styles you would like to correct. I think the power of observation is potent, as well as the candor of conversations."

As the director of the Peace Corps, he had the opportunity to visit colleges and campuses talking about the Peace Corps and met with university presidents, chancellors, and deans. His visits led him to view this sector much differently than before. He realized many of his own values aligned with that of higher education.

"So, I really had an interesting view of the sector and how it's mission oriented, values centered, and thought it would be interesting," Gearan said as I continued to dig deeper.

He remembered telling his mentor Donna Shalala, then-chancellor of University of Wisconsin-Madison, that he would like to be a college president someday during a visit in 1992, right before Clinton's election.

"She was a great conversant with me about these kinds of things," Gearan said.

While attending Harvard's Graduate School of Education for a seminar for new presidents, the faculty member who ran the program became an important mentor to him. She was a great mentor who had an understanding of higher education.

As I listened, it made me think how his first great mentor was his mother, and in the two critical professional roles as the Director of the Peace Corps and President of Hobart and William Smith, he had two women who were essential in his development. These two women helped him understand the importance of strategic thinking, planning and execution. The lessons they taught him were the necessity of leadership, listening, and sound decision making. The importance of what we call today as self-care and how not to lose your sense of balance of other life responsibilities by making sure you keep the right balance.

"Mentors can come at different stages of one's life," he said. "But generally, you have to then rewind the tape and see how things fit in. And then I think there are different kinds of mentorships for different stages in life. Right?"

I nodded, lost in contemplation about my time as a college student and how appreciative I was that he had taken me under his wing as a protege.

He entered my life at a certain point and is still there for me. By merely coaching me and giving me exposure, he helped pave the way for my achievement. In my view, exposure mentoring essentially involves introducing individuals to various options granting them entry to new tools, knowledge, or even positions of leadership.

"So do you think exposure mentorship is a useful solution to help companies with diversity, equity, inclusion?" I asked him with the intention of discovering how we replicate our experience for others on a similar road.

"Not everyone grew up at the kitchen table talking about X, Y, or Z field, right?" Gearan said as he eloquently showcased his extensive knowledge and understanding on the importance of mentorship and its relationship with DEI. He continued his thought as I leaned closer to my MacBook Pro screen. "So how do you expose sectors of the economy, roles in organizations, the ecosystems of different professions? It's through that exposure, and this needs to be turbocharged for this next century. Given the challenges we have in our country, and given the structural barriers that exist, particularly for people of color, how do we accelerate this in ways that take stock of the rooted nature of some of these obstacles and break some of those barriers down?"

His answer was connected directly to his point earlier about observation. Observing styles and opportunities offer people exposure they may not typically receive.

"When you look at people, there are exceptions, but frequently individuals go into the same professional spaces as their families," Gearan said.

I couldn't agree more with President Gearan's statement. I know friends who ended up becoming nurses because that is what their mothers, aunts, and sisters have done. I also know folks who became attorneys because their dad, mother, or relative was one. His comment reinforced my prejudiced belief that we often become what we see.

President Gearan continued, "Like dentists, business owners, lawyers, teachers, and doctors—if you've seen that and you say, 'I think I wanna be a dentist. My uncle was a dentist,' that's exposure. They grew up at the kitchen table talking about teaching second grade because that's what their mother or father did, or funeral director, or whatever it is."

"Yes!" I shouted, for I knew he understood the remarkable benefits exposure has in one's life and how the lack of exposure can serve as negative consequences. His insightful perspective truly resonated with me, and I appreciated the depth of his response.

As President Gearan slightly tilted his head, he continued his response. "But exposure is also bringing that kitchen table broadly to those who—even though you do have a second-grade-teacher mother—can be exposed to what it's like working in a financial consulting firm or in higher education."

I said, "I love 'at the kitchen table' because it's so, so true."

Later that evening, while having dinner with my wife and kids, I wanted to be intentional with our dinner talks. As we blessed our food, we held hands. I couldn't stop thinking about Mark Gearan's interview. As a father, it was now my duty to broaden my kids' horizons. The greater I expose them, the more probable it is they will lead a meaningful life.

FINAL REFLECTION

An important caveat: I do not recommend asking someone to mentor you without doing your research.

In my case, it underscores the value of courage in pursuing opportunities of growth. Sometimes we overthink and talk ourselves out from a decision that can change our lives or prevent personal and professional growth.

The concept of "exposure mentorship" emerges as a significant theme. The mentor introducing you to various opportunities, events, and influential individuals showcases the role of exposure in broadening perspectives and fostering growth. This form of mentorship goes beyond traditional guidance and actively involves mentees in real-world experiences, helping them navigate different aspects of life and leadership.

My suggestion for you is to find a mentor who exceeds your expectations. In any company or organization, I implore you to build a team of mentors who can help support your personal and professional development. Even if the mentor is not aligned in your field of interest, just be sure they align with your values and truly believe in you.

CHAPTER 3

The Language of Success: Mastering Code-Switching for Professional Growth

Adapt and adopt are not the same! While both terms involve some form of change or acceptance, "adapt" refers to the process of adjusting to changes or new conditions, while "adopt" refers to the act of taking on or accepting something, such as a practice or idea. Adding these two behaviors to your toolkit allows you to navigate any work environment you may find yourself in. I didn't know the difference between the two for many years, and at the time it wasn't relevant.

It was challenging to be the best version of myself until an intervention allowed me to adjust to a new environment. It started one morning after being sent to the principal's office.

"Go to in-school detention!" My teacher shouted at me. Here I was, yet again, in trouble. I was angry at my teacher for sending me to the main office to serve my time with the principal, mostly because on this particular day, Wendy and Jim were visiting me at my middle school in Newark.

They're not going to want to take me after seeing me at the principal office, I thought as I sat in the chair, swinging my legs back and forth to distract myself. My chances were now ruined to become the Fresh Prince of Geneva.

I continued in my thoughts, perplexed and upset. The pairs of Jordans, the clothes, the video games, and the opportunity of living away from the hood are now gone. Fortunately for me, Wendy and Jim did not renege on their promise. The silver lining was they knew what they were getting themselves into when they saw me.

My seventh through twelfth grade years were an adjustment, but the show *The Fresh Prince of Bel-Air* kept me grounded in how to make the best of my situation of living away from home. It took some getting used to with the silent nights growing up in Geneva, but by my second year, it became my way of life. I was able to put my guard down while walking the streets of Geneva; I couldn't do that while walking to school in Newark and passing by crowds of drug dealers. I missed my family tremendously, but I kept my eyes on the prize, which was graduating from high school and going off to college.

I never felt I had to assimilate to Wendy and Jim's culture. They allowed me to be myself; however, living among them, I noticed how I adapted to the different rooms I entered in with ease.

Growing up, I loved the *The Fresh Prince of Bel-Air*, which was a popular American sitcom that originally aired from

1990 to 1996. The show follows the life of a young man named Will Smith, played by Will Smith, who is sent from his working-class neighborhood in Philadelphia to live with his wealthy aunt and uncle in their upscale Bel-Air mansion in Los Angeles. Will had to adjust to his new lifestyle in this wealthy and predominantly African American neighborhood.

In the show, his fun-loving and street-smart personality often clashed with his strict and sophisticated Aunt Vivian and Uncle Phil. We see Will Smith's character navigate between different social contexts and adapt to his surroundings. He demonstrates this through his language, behavior, and mannerisms.

He switches between different linguistic or cultural codes depending on the situation, environment, or audience.

I did not really understand what Will was doing until after I relocated from Newark to Geneva. He was code-switching.

Before Will moved to Bel-Air, he spoke in a more informal and slang-filled manner. Once he moved to the affluent neighborhood of Bel-Air, he adapted his language to be more formal and appropriate for the upscale setting. He adjusted his grammar, speech patterns, and even his vocabulary. His behavior and mannerism shifted to fit in this social class.

Will also adjusted his behavior and mannerisms by learning the proper etiquette, social norms, and customs of his new wealthy community. This included adopting a more polished and refined demeanor, adhering to dress codes and displaying appropriate table manners when dining with Aunt Vivian, Uncle Phil, and other high-society individuals.

We also see the opposite of Will Smith's character in Carlton Banks. Carlton had "nerdy tendencies," lacked street knowledge, had a more rigid personality, and adhered to the rules. But in one episode, we see Carlton become more like Will Smith, being able to code-switch and explain financial advice to gangsters, such as how to open a Charles Schwab account.

Of course, this episode emphasizes stereotypes based on how one dresses, but in the episode, the stereotypes were dismantled by the fact that Carlton could dress the part and still navigate the room effectively. Some would even say his ability to speak and behave in a manner the gangsters understood allowed them to be more receptive and take heed of the financial wisdom. Either way, what we see between these two characters is the ability to code-switch.

Code-switching refers to the practice of alternating between different languages, dialects, or cultural norms in communication. It involves adjusting one's linguistic and cultural behavior to fit different social contexts or situations. Code-switching can happen within a single conversation or even within a single sentence, as individuals switch between different codes or linguistic forms. These can be verbal cues or nonverbal cues, such as body language or dress.

George Paasewe, author of *How Black College Students Learn Code-Switching* defined code-switching in his interview with the *Milwaukee Journal Sentinel* as "the practice of adjusting one's style of speech, appearance, behavior and expression to a particular context or situation."[1]

Importantly, code-switching should be done authentically and respectfully. It should not be used to demean or belittle any language or culture. Awareness of the power dynamics and potential biases associated with code-switching is crucial, as it can reflect broader societal expectations and inequalities. Ultimately, the decision to code-switch should be based on context, the individuals involved, and your own comfort level and judgment.

I was fortunate to never feel the need to code-switch while living with Wendy and Jim. I continued to dress the same, wearing my hoodies, baggy jeans, and Timberlands. I continued to listen to hip hop and wore my new fitted baseball cap however I wanted.

But when it came to writing essays, I received critical feedback on grammar and understood the importance of speaking and writing so the world in which I lived could respect and understand me. We exchanged our cultures. They were as interested in my history as I was in theirs. We had genuine conversations as to why I needed to wear a durag at night and how I brushed my hair to maintain the waves. They were not there to judge, but to guide and help me find my way in this world.

Code-switching first happened to me at Hobart and William Smith Colleges, and I didn't even realize it was happening. It was not something I was taught, and it was not done in a way to change who I was. During my time working in President Mark Gearan's office, I was unaware of the office dress code. I would show up with my colorful Coogi sweater, baggy jeans, and Timberland boots. President Gearan never pulled me aside to say, "Hey Dan, I love your style, but your outfit for the office should look more like this." I felt proud of my culture and do not think I would have even accepted it if he told me that.

One evening as a student trustee, we the board members attended a board dinner meeting at a local restaurant in downtown Geneva. I was nervous I did not know proper etiquette on how to interact with wealthy people and worried I would stick out like a red dot on an all-white painting—especially regarding how I spoke. There, I saw Bill Whitaker, a smooth gentleman who gracefully walked into the room. His thick mustache reminded me of Alex Trebek on Jeopardy. Everyone greeted him with a big smile.

"Hi, Bill. You made it!" another board of trustees member shouted across the room as they shook his hand.

Bill had on a long, black Burberry trench coat in the middle of winter. This was my first time seeing a Black man in a Burberry trench coat. He was the first Black man I met who was a millionaire. He had class, culture, and confidence. He dressed well. This was the moment I realized I needed to polish my appearance and dress appropriately for the different rooms I would be invited to.

Bill Whitaker served as a north star for me for a very long time as someone who looked like me and garnered much success. I was only twenty years old at the time, but I knew I wanted to be in a position like him to make an impact in the world based on his work and his role as a member of the colleges' board of trustees. Bill is an American television journalist and correspondent on the *CBS News* program *60 Minutes*.

I began to understand I am not being a phony or a sell-out in adopting different social norms, dress codes, or communication patterns when interacting with individuals from different cultural backgrounds. Code-switching can be used in multicultural or multilingual environments, where people have to navigate between different cultural or linguistic groups. It can be driven by the desire to establish rapport, avoid misunderstandings, or conform to social expectations.

Code-switching can have both positive and negative implications. It can facilitate effective communication, bridge cultural gaps, and promote inclusivity. It allows individuals to connect with different communities and to navigate diverse social settings. However, code-switching can also be a result of societal pressures, discrimination, or the need to conform, which may have emotional or psychological impacts on individuals.

I want to be clear; this was not my first time seeing a Black man dress up. My father, Pastor Rosmond De Nose, would wear dress pants, a dress shirt, and a blazer even on his days off. I was also accustomed to business casual attire and dressing up for special days and events, but something clicked when I saw Bill Whitaker. It all made sense how the world can view you based on how you dress and speak, and if you know how to adjust your speech to be understood, it will work in your favor.

WHEN SHOULD I CODE-SWITCH?

Six examples or common instances when code-switching may be appropriate are as follows:

- Multilingual environments: If you are fluent in multiple languages, you may code-switch between languages when conversing with individuals who understand those languages. This can help facilitate effective communication and create a sense of connection with others who share the same linguistic background.
- Professional settings: Code-switching can be valuable in professional settings, especially when adapting to different communication styles, levels of formality, or industry-specific jargon. Adjusting your language and behavior to match the professional context can help you establish rapport and effectively convey your ideas.
- Cultural contexts: In diverse cultural contexts, code-switching may be necessary to navigate social norms, etiquette, and customs. Adapting your behavior, greetings, or communication patterns to align with the cultural expectations of a particular setting can help you establish connections and show respect for the cultural practices of others.
- Social groups or communities: Code-switching may occur when interacting with different social groups or communities that have their own unique language, slang, or cultural references. Adjusting your language or mannerisms to fit in and be understood within a particular group can promote social cohesion and a sense of belonging.
- Academic or professional disciplines: In specialized fields or academic disciplines, code-switching may involve

using specific terminology, concepts, or methodologies that are unique to that discipline. This allows for effective communication within the field and demonstrates expertise and understanding of the subject matter.

- Personal relationships: Code-switching can also be relevant in personal relationships, particularly when navigating different social circles or adapting to the communication styles of individuals with varying backgrounds or preferences. Adjusting your language and behavior in these situations can promote understanding and strengthen a more authentic and meaningful connection with those around you.

The first time I code-switched was at a fundraiser the college organized called "Campaign for Colleges." I was invited to be a student speaker for the fundraiser. My hair was in the process of turning into dreadlocks, and I wore a tuxedo. When I wrote my speech, I drafted it in a way my audience would understand. I did not use slang or cultural words only my friends and I would understand. I limited the colloquialisms and made it as plain as I could so my audience would not get lost in translation. It was only a five-minute speech about my experience as a student. The folks in the room loved it, and afterward all were interested in taking photos with me.

In reflection, I understand many people may have their opinions about this concept of code-switching and believe we should not have to conform. I agree; the concept is what you make of it and how you use it. Being genuine in who you are at all times is the key. The character of who you are should remain the same. Learn from your mentor so you too can take advantage of the different rooms you occupy.

When a mentor brings you along to expose you to Wall Street, I recommend you learn the language so you can speak their language. When a mentor invites you to attend a black-tie event, I recommend you attend and watch the dynamics of those in position so you can understand how to do the same when you are in the room without them. When a mentor invites you attend a classroom of seventh graders, I recommend you learn the educational terms so you can succeed as a teacher.

The point of all of this is, as a mentee, you must learn, grow, and apply lessons when you see fit, and always remember to share what you have learned with others. Some people may never get the opportunity to have access to the rooms you have access to, so pay it forward and give back by teaching others.

As a mentor, you can play a crucial role in helping mentees navigate and excel in various environments through code-switching by teaching them the following:

- Cultural work awareness: while the mentee grasps the nuances of communication, a mentor might offer insights into the cultural norms and expectations within various professional settings.
- Professional language vocabulary guide: help the mentee create a professional vocabulary that works in a variety of settings, including industry events, team meetings, and client meetings.
- Behavioral observation and input: give the mentee feedback on their behavior in different settings, offering guidance on how to adapt their demeanor, body language, and communication style appropriately.

- Navigating conflicts: offer advice on how to resolve disputes or conflicts in a way that respects the workplace culture of the particular setting.
- Dress code and etiquette: provide guidance on acceptable attire and business etiquette for various situations, such as formal meetings, relaxed office settings, or industry-specific events.

Mentors play a role in grooming the next generation of leaders. Through exposure mentorship, mentees are better equipped to assume leadership roles and to contribute to the success and adaptability of their organizations. Mentors contribute significantly to a mentee's ability to navigate diverse professional environments. The guidance, support, and insights provided by mentors empower mentees to adapt, communicate effectively, and achieve success in a wide range of settings throughout their careers.

Although we may not all be able to relocate to Geneva or become a Fresh Prince or Princess, we have the opportunity to learn the same valuable lessons as those who have the privilege of being taught this. Our best way of doing so is through the power of exposure mentorship.

FINAL LESSONS

Code-switching is a valuable skill, particularly in multicultural or multilingual environments, as it allows individuals to adapt their language and behavior to fit different social contexts. It is important to approach code-switching with authenticity and respect, cautioning against its misuse for demeaning purposes. The exploration of both positive and negative implications recognizes code-switching's role in effective communication while acknowledging the potential impact on individuals due to societal pressures.

A pivotal realization about the significance of code-switching was during the encounter with Bill Whitaker, a successful Black man serving as a role model. In specific situations such as work, board meetings, or formal events, you may find yourself having to code-switch. When that happens, just like it was mentioned in the previous chapter, you need to be yourself.

Code-switching should not compromise authenticity; instead, it empowers professionals to bring their authentic selves to various professional settings. Mentors play a pivotal role in encouraging mentees to embrace their uniqueness while imparting the skills needed to adapt when necessary, fostering authentic leadership.

I encourage you to embrace learning, growth, and the application of code-switching when appropriate. Mentors help you in guiding through cultural awareness, professional language, behavioral adaptation, conflict resolution, dress code, and etiquette. Every workforce has its own culture and climate, and having a mentor in the organization that you decide to work in can provide important advice on what is appropriate.

In essence, I implore you to genuinely understand and apply code-switching as a skill to excel in various settings while staying true to your identity.

CHAPTER 4

Small Moments, Big Impact: Building Mentor-Mentee Relationships

Exposure mentorship is not only found in an agreed mentor-mentee relationship but also in experiences.

In a world where conventional mentorship paradigms often take center stage, it is crucial to recognize the significance of exposure mentorship—a form of guidance where we live vicariously through our mentors. Unlike structured mentor-mentee relationships, exposure mentorship emerges when we least expect it. We are beckoned to embrace the profound lessons embedded in every experience, urging us to learn from those who may unintentionally guide us in our decision making through conversation or moments shared.

What makes exposure mentorship so significant? Think of exposure mentorship as a magical potion that helps us go beyond what we expect, like pushing us to try new things and get comfortable with the unknown. It's like an invitation to attend the premiere of a private screening. It's not just about mentors providing guidance; it's about the mentee having extra support during tough times. Those impactful brainstorming sessions happen when no one else is around.

During my first year on campus, I befriended a student named Katie who also lived in New Jersey. She offered to carpool with me during our holiday breaks. Like most college students would, I jumped at the opportunity to save money so I could enjoy the weekend with my roommates. I could not refuse an opportunity to save on purchasing a bus ticket.

The ride from the Geneva was always a beautiful experience. In the fall, I appreciated the dazzling array of orange, yellow, red, and sometimes purple pigments. The winter covered us with an arctic windshield that made me question whether human beings were truly capable of living in the cold. Our conversations were always pleasant. I would offer gas money, but she always refused. The following year, her father was picking me up halfway and dropping me off in Newark.

"Hi Dan, I will be there in ten minutes to pick you up," he texted. They had invited me to dinner.

I was on my winter break in 2010 and sitting in my parents' living room watching the news about the Haiti earthquake. We were busy making calls to check in on our family back in the homeland to make sure they were okay. Because of that, I wanted to stay home a while longer, but my family insisted I should go.

Katie's parents, Mr. and Mrs. H, had invited me over for dinner, an experience that would shape my future. When I arrived, they introduced me to Katie's friend, Nordia. Like me, she had Caribbean ancestry. The mood proved relaxing and helped take my mind off the global situation.

When it came time for me to leave, Mr. H drove me home. I decided to tell him about my life, who I was, where I came from. He was blown away by my life experiences and said, "Dan, I would like to stay in touch with you. Please let me know if I can do anything to support you."

Like most young college students, I lacked the skills to follow up on that, but I told him, "Yes, I'll do that."

I really did not have a clue as to my plans after college. How would I use my degree to position myself in the race of life? My significant student loans and the accompanying interest would cripple me if I did not land on my feet and go straight into the workforce. I knew what I had to do, and said to myself, "Since I always had a passion for the military, why not join the army?" Knowing my grandfather was a military man in Haiti and my brother Osborn served in the Navy, I felt maybe this would be my path.

I was just one semester away from graduating. If you were around during the 2010s, you probably remember the job market was daunting and many people were looking for employment. When I told Mr. H about my intentions, he did not agree or disagree.

He simply said, "I want you to meet my good friend, Mr. B."

Spring break was coming, and I had no concrete plans besides returning home to Newark to spend time with my family.

My phone rang. "Hi, Dan."

"Hi, Mr. H," I responded, a bit surprised but happy to hear from him.

"Mr. B was able to coordinate a day for you to meet with some of his colleagues. I am going to connect the two of you so he can go over the plan with you."

Mr. H had worked with Mr. B for many years at Prudential in Newark. Mr. H had been the chief compliance officer, and Mr. B was the chief learning officer, advising the chairman and senior business leaders on talent management, organizational structure, and the design of learning and leadership development strategies.

I tried my best not to show how eager I was for this opportunity, but I could not resist. I shouted with an astounded voice, "Thank you!"

I soon gave Mr. B a call, and he walked me through his plan.

He said, "Are you able to get to downtown Newark by 8:00 a.m.?"

I did not have a car at the time, but I had no issue taking the bus. I told him, "Absolutely! I will be there."

The day arrived, and I put my best suit on. I was going to meet with the leaders of a Fortune 500 company. My parents told me they would drop me off and to pray before I left. As the car stopped at a red light on Springfield Ave, I thought of all the lessons I learned during my time as a student trustee at Hobart and William Smith. I kept reminding myself I was qualified to meet with these people and I was deserving of this opportunity. I felt self-doubt creeping and to silence the noise of insecurity, I continued to boost my confidence by telling myself, "Dan, you deserve to be there!"

When I arrived at Prudential, flags of different countries waved in the air. I could see the high level of professionalism as folks entered the building. The guard welcomed me in as I provided him with my ID. He told me I was on the list and asked me to wait.

It was not long before, I heard my name called. "Hi, Dan. My name is Chrissy. I work with Mr. B. He asked if I could come down and get you."

I stood up with a big smile and greeted her with a handshake. "Thank you for getting me," I said.

Mr. B was in his corner office. I'd never been in an office so big before. He left his desk and came over with a wide smile. "It's great to finally meet you in person. We have much planned ahead of us, but it will all be great. Do you want to leave anything in my office before we begin?"

I told him I brought extra copies of resumes with me.

He said, "Great. You can bring them with you."

The first meeting he had coordinated was with a woman named Mary O'Malley who ultimately changed my life. She still serves as a mentor and has transcended into a sponsor. Five years after meeting Mary, she sponsored my first fundraising event to help build my nonprofit, and she donated one thousand dollars. It was the first check to enter my organization's bank account.

Interestingly enough, I did not know what a sponsor was back then, but after interviewing a woman named Ms. DB, who works for one of the big five global leading accounting firms, she shared with me her definition of what a sponsor was and the impact her sponsor had on her. She defined it as "someone who has the authority to make change. Someone who has a seat at tables you do not have a seat at. Someone who is willing to use their political capital to help you advance your career—because some mentors don't have that authority, and some mentors don't have a seat at the table."

Mentors assist us in developing our individual skills by listening to our problems and offering their advice. Sponsors, on the other hand, assist us in getting the next gig. They are the people who will discuss you when you are not present and argue your case. Mary O'Malley served as a mentor and sponsor, and many others during my time at Prudential did the same.

Every professional I met during my time at Prudential exuded leadership qualities that mirrored those I encountered during my days as a student in college. I observed a level of confidence in their interactions with their colleagues.

"What is it that makes these individuals so special?" I wondered. Is it sheer will mixed with a tenacious goal of success? Maybe they read a book or learned a life lesson from their parents. If I never had the chance again to connect with these high-level leaders, I would gain knowledge through observing them.

I was nervous my Newark-Geneva accent would make me sound unprofessional when speaking to the people I met. This was not the case. These individuals were willing to listen to me. Even for the brief moments we shared, I felt their care, for it seemed like they had already agreed to mentor me. Although I did not ask them to assume this role, I asked them for their business cards. They agreed, and I have remained in contact with all of them to this day.

Mr. B, Mary O'Malley, Mr. H, and many others taught me a valuable lesson. Mentors and sponsors are necessary when you are on the path to becoming great in your career and in life. It is these individuals who are able to unlock doors you may have never known existed. They are often behind the scenes, providing guidance and exposure to allow you the opportunities of growth and success. My interview with Ms. DB reminded me how the right person can give you the keys to enter rooms of authority, leadership, and decision-making roles.

My good friend Innis had connected me with his colleague Ms. DB who worked in diversity, equity, and inclusion. This interview was critical as I continued on my quest of understanding how mentorship can impact DEI within an organization.

On the day of the interview, my wife, children, and I were heading down to Maryland for spring break. The Airbnb we decided to stay in was the perfect place to host the virtual interview.

"Babe," my wife Devonne said, "we will give you privacy and stay outside so we don't interrupt your interview."

I thanked her and quickly grabbed my laptop and ran up the front stairs to the house.

I set up my laptop and waited. Once my interviewee arrived, I jumped right into the questioning. I asked, "What was the critical moment in your life when you needed a mentor?"

"In my first three years at my firm, I realized it was going to be extremely difficult for me. Because if you can imagine thirty years ago, if we feel like we're one in any room setting, I was one in ten room settings at that time. There were very, very little ethnically diverse professionals at the company at that time.

"I knew I would need help to advance my career. I was very young. I didn't really have a lot of experience around what it meant to be in a corporate organization. I was the first in my family to actually work in a corporate organization. We didn't sit around the table and talk about, 'Hey, what do you do when you get there?'"

As I listened, I could see the parallel between our lives. She too recognized the importance of mentorship and guidance, and how seeking individuals who could provide valuable insights and support.

"I was very green," she said. "I knew I would need help from someone who had a seat at the table, who had the authority to make change. At that time, I knew I had to build relationships with someone who would be able to help me advance my career. At the time, I thought that was a mentor, but what I learned later on in my career is that there is a distinct difference between having a mentor and having someone as a sponsor."

She continued. "So, a mentor for me is someone I can confide in, someone with whom I have a really good relationship who will tell me, 'Hey, no, you can't do that,' or, 'You can do that,' and be very honest with me about directions. It's someone I look up to because they've done what I've done and someone who will be there for me to provide advice and guidance."

I pondered these words for a moment, realizing the significance of mentors in her journey.

"But a sponsor for me is someone who has the authority to make change. Someone who has a seat at tables that you do not have a seat at. Someone who is willing to use their political capital to help you advance your career. And so, I think that's very different, right? Because some mentors don't have that authority and some mentors don't have a seat at the table, but they can provide advice and guidance and be there to listen and be there for you when you need them."

The distinction hit home, prompting me to look within while recognizing the pivotal role of sponsors in navigating the corridors of influence and impact within my professional realm.

"So three years into my career, I realized I needed a sponsor. I had to figure out how I would go about building a relationship with someone who was a sponsor, and get that person to feel comfortable enough to use their political capital for me to advance my career."

What Ms. DB shared with me helped me realize Mr. B was both a mentor and a sponsor. He helped guide me through some very difficult decisions as a mentor, but as a sponsor he and his wife gave me my first car. It was a red 1994 Honda Accord in mint condition. He is also the reason why I received my first job out of college.

During a specific period in my adulthood, I faced a decision that would significantly alter my life. The stakes were high, and I felt overwhelmed trying to figure out what to do. In that moment, he patiently guided me over the phone on the art of decision-making. Rather than making the decision for me, he imparted his process of critical decision-making. I learned the importance of keeping the end goal in mind and weighing the options to minimize negative impacts. As a result, the best decision was made, and the journey since then has led me to a wonderful place. I owe many thanks to Mr. B for his selfless acts of kindness and support throughout my early career.

Every conversation I had with Mr. B made me feel like a student learning from a great professor. The initial connection between the two of us was through his friend Mr. H, but the relationship I fostered was intentionally done through time spent over lunch, coffee, and after-work phone calls, when I needed genuine advice on how to navigate my career.

The best relationships between mentor and mentee are not forced. It is the small moments and interactions made in the present moment.

I returned for my second career day with Mr. B, which is something I will never forget. My charcoal-gray suit was put with a white shirt and a colorful peach, green, purple, and black striped tie. My family drove down to City Hall, and my stomach was in knots. I tried my best to compose myself, but all I could think about was meeting the Mayor of Newark.

Mayor Cory Booker at the time was up for reelection as the thirty-eighty mayor of Newark, New Jersey. He was all over national news for many reasons during his first term, and based on what the media portrayed, he continued his efforts to become nationally recognized as one of the most influential African American politicians.

Mr. B waited for me in the lobby. "Dan." He waved me over.

As we exited the elevator to the second floor, we were greeted by a police officer outside the mayor's office. Mr. B led the way through the door and told the receptionist we were there for our meeting. We did not wait long. Mr. B asked me how I felt, and I told him I was excited. In the meeting, both Mayor Booker's chief of staff, Mo Butler, and his senior advisor, DeShawn Wright, were present in the room, warmly welcoming me with friendly smiles as they stood.

Mayor Booker asked, "So Dan, tell me, where do you see yourself in twenty years?"

I told him I saw myself running my own nonprofit, working with students.

He laughed, and said, "When I was your age, I had no clue what I would be doing in twenty years."

The meeting didn't last long. DeShawn walked us to the door. I stopped and asked for his business card.

A couple of months later, I received a phone call that Mayor Booker wanted me to work for him as his body aide.

It was one of the best days of my life. My time working with Cory Booker was transformational. I was there when Oprah's film crew came to Newark. I rode in the car with Gayle King. I was privy to private conversations and served as one of his points of contact. When founder of Facebook, Mark Zuckerberg, donated one hundred million dollars to Newark, I was there. Before every event, I had to brief him on his talking points. I ran alongside him to chase down a criminal one Saturday morning.

In my role, I had a front row seat to witness effective leadership and what was required when making tough decisions. I had to remain grounded and focus on what is important: serving the people. Countless times, when cameras were not around, I saw Cory's character. He is one of the humblest people I've known and a true servant leader.

Although Cory Booker was not officially asked to be my mentor, my time with him was a form of exposure mentorship. He gave me the confidence to believe I am capable of doing anything I set my mind to. Entering the role, I was not sure of my value or self-worth in terms of being an effective leader. In reflection, I discovered I did not give myself enough grace. I was focused on rushing the process of being the best me as possible and did not focus as much on my progress.

One late evening, as I laid in bed exhausted from being in my third week on the job, I contemplated how helpful I was to the mayor. He was a person who had a photographic memory, was a national hero who had saved someone from a burning building, and had attended Oxford University. I felt intimidated, especially as a recent graduate from college in my first role. It was hard for me to understand how to be effective to someone who had achieved so much.

Like most ambitious people, I took my role seriously and with a level of pride that I was able to work with the mayor. It was a daily struggle to memorize all the details I could about his daily schedule. His prior body aide, Sharon, was considered a rockstar whom everyone loved. She transitioned from his body aide in the field to being the one to keep his office and personal life running smoothly. She was excellent at what she did for him.

As I continued to lay in bed thinking of who could show me how to be great in my role, my phone illuminated the room with a text. "Who is texting me this late?" I wondered as I grabbed my phone to see what the emergency was. It was Cory Booker, and the text was motivational. He concluded his message by saying, "I am like Batman, and you are my Robin."

From that point forward, I realized no matter what came my way in this role, I needed to act with confidence and not be scared to fail. The prospect of failure was a deterrent to performing at the high level I believed I was capable of. I was so concerned about making mistakes I forgot to breathe and concentrate on doing what I was doing correctly. This is a lesson I've taken with me in all my roles: confidence and believing you can accomplish something is fifty percent of the job. The remaining fifty percent is divided into two parts: learning your role and simply executing. Go forward and don't be frightened of what might go wrong; rather, think about what will go wrong if you don't try.

Cory Booker and my great mentors are part of the building blocks of the legacy I will leave behind through my nonprofit. I wanted to replicate the experience of exposure for students who may not have been as lucky as me. I believe with the right exposure, anyone can come across the right opportunity to achieve their dreams.

FINAL LESSON

There is power in seizing opportunities, especially when it comes to mentorship.

The encounter with Mr. H exemplifies the impact of personal connections in shaping one's future. While mentors offer advice and guidance, sponsors, with their authority, open doors and advocate for their mentees' career advancement. The story reflects the importance of these relationships in navigating the complexities of your professional life.

The lessons learned from my mentors and sponsors, along with exposure to diverse experiences, became foundational elements in my pursuit of creating my nonprofit to provide similar opportunities for future generations.

Consider your journey as a collection of diverse puzzle pieces. At times, the connections may not make sense in the present, but as you persist along your path, these pieces will gradually transform into a meaningful whole through which the picture will become clear. The potential of the right connections can indeed be life-altering.

Empower yourself by crafting a list of three inspiring leaders you aspire to emulate. Take bold action, and approach them with a sincere request for mentorship. If their schedules don't permit mentoring, express gratitude and maintain regular contact. Witness the incredible impact this authentic initiative can have, benefiting both you and them in unexpected ways.

The journey culminates in a profound realization: mentors and sponsors are the keys to unlocking doors we may not know exist. Their guidance, support, and exposure become the building blocks of a lasting legacy. The lessons learned from mentors and sponsors, coupled with exposure to diverse experiences, shape a narrative that emphasizes the importance of these relationships in navigating the complexities of one's professional life.

As you reflect on this chapter, recognize the puzzle pieces of your journey. Connections may not always make sense in the present but will persist along your path. Craft a list of inspiring leaders, and take bold action to seek their mentorship. The blueprint for success lies in your ability to embrace opportunities, empower yourself, and forge connections that can be truly transformative. The potential of these connections is immense, altering the course of your life in ways you might not foresee. Seize the opportunity, embark on this journey, and witness the extraordinary impact it can have on your personal and professional growth.

CHAPTER 5

The Mentoring Effect: Strategic Alliances for Impactful Mentorships

Who are your allies? Choose wisely!

Your allies should share similar values and goals. This alignment ensures your mentorship and partnership efforts are focused on common objectives, creating a more harmonious and effective collaboration.

Having the right allies is about creating a foundation built on credibility, resources, and a commitment to positive impact. Thoughtful selection of allies enhances the effectiveness, sustainability, and overall success of mentorship, self-development, and initiatives that support transitioning into the workforce.

Strategic allies bring diverse expertise and resources to the table. Whether it's knowledge, experience, or financial support, having allies with complementary strengths can enrich your programs and professional skills development by providing valuable insights and support.

Have you ever wondered why successful influencers in social media businesses are able to thrive better than others? Yes, being a great storyteller, being interactive with your audience, and having engaging content make a huge difference. But what brings them the revenue of success is largely due to their collaborations.

Collaborations with other influencers or brands can greatly expand an influencer's reach. Successful influencers actively identify alliances that complement their brand and resonate with their target audience, resulting in mutually beneficial interactions. It's all about making sensible decisions.

The same is true when it comes to establishing mentorship ties and company collaborations. You must form an alliance and collaborate with folks who share your vision. For individuals in the passenger seat looking for mentorship, the technique works: form alliances.

I heard the speaker say, "If you can see it, you can be it." The quote was famously made by the tennis legend and founder of the Women's Sports Foundation, Billie Jean King. She underlined the necessity for girls to be encouraged by witnessing other women and girls participate in sports. This quote remains true and stand the test of time, not only for girls but for all people.

As I looked throughout a sea of people attending the 2023 National Mentoring Summit, I saw a wave of mentors representing their state. But more importantly, they were people who believed in a just cause to mentor a generation. This was not the first time I had heard this quote; however, this was the time it impacted me the strongest. My experiences have allowed me to understand our network is our net worth, and as a mentor once said to me, "It is not only who you know, but it is also who knows you."

The purpose of attending this summit was to sharpen my skills as the executive director of Leaders of the 21st Century, to learn from some of the best in their fields, to network, and to figure out how to create a diverse pipeline of effective leaders to enter the workforce. My quest was to discover if exposure mentorship could in fact level the playing field for employment in the twenty-first century. In other words, is it possible to create a bridge toward upward mobility?

I knew this would be the place to gain knowledge. I would return better at serving the young people of my organization with new insights and strategies on how to become employed or gain access to internships in the career field of their choice.

Later that night, I spent time reflecting and thinking about the quote. I thought of my first example of being exposed to a Black male leader. It was my father.

My father founded a school in Haiti and became a pastor. I remember watching him lead at a young age and witnessed how he was an effective servant leader. I thought about some of my other mentors who were Black men, like a gentleman named Dan McNeal who was introduced to me by Mary O'Malley. She felt I needed mentors who looked like me.

Dan and I connected during my career day at Prudential, and he has mentored me since my senior year in college.

He has always been consistent and in many ways demonstrated a caliber of qualities that makes him a perfect mentor: relatability, honesty, patience, strong morals, consistency, empathy. He is a great man who speaks on my behalf when I am not in the room.

My thoughts continued as I considered my third job after college as a deputy director of community advocacy, led by a mentor, Eric Stevenson. He was a great executive director, and many of the lessons I learned from him were through watching and listening. He serves as my executive coach, and I owe much of my leadership skills as an executive director to him. He would always say, "In order to have progress, you have to go through the process." Here I was, going through a process I had chosen in hopes of making our world a better place, especially for those of us who have been disenfranchised.

The next morning, I took advantage of the cool morning breeze and walked from my hotel over to the conference location. I wanted to make sure I arrived in time to hear the morning speakers. As I walked inside, I overheard someone speaking about the mentoring effect.

I had never heard of this before. I decided to do a quick search and discovered it was a national survey commissioned by the organization MENTOR. It was the first nationally representative survey of young people on the topic of both informal and formal mentoring. It was also a literature and landscape review and had insights from a variety of key leaders in business, philanthropy, government, and education.

The survey found 1.8 million young adults facing risks had been matched in mentoring relationships through mentoring programs while they grew up. It states despite the positive upward trend, one in three young people surveyed did not have a mentor while they were growing up. It projected sixteen million young people, including nine million young people facing risks, will reach adulthood without connecting with a mentor of any kind.[1]

The question remains: how do we build this pipeline of diverse candidates to positively impact an organization's diversity, equity, and inclusion profile? A few months after the conference, I reached out to a mentor of mine, Ron Andrews, former vice president of US businesses and head of human resources at Prudential Financial. I asked him his thoughts on how we can improve DEI in corporate America.

He said, "You don't know what you can be until you start to see it."

Those of us who have the privilege to know Ron all say the same thing. He is trustworthy, a man of integrity, wise, cheerful, and honest. His opinion matters and his legacy continues to thrive at Prudential here in Newark. A merit-based scholarship was named after him in 2020, the Ron Andrews Diversity Scholarship (RADS) Program, which was designed to help advance diversity in the asset management industry. It is the foundation of Black Leadership Forum (BLF), which is the largest resource group within the company and the most influential.

What he was able to do in his position of authority happened in two parts. He gave people insight on where they needed to be in their career and tips on what they needed to do to get there. He focused on the whole person and on how their decisions could impact their lives. The BLF platform served as a means of helping people within the group with mentors. For many, this gave them the platform to showcase their talent to be recognized as effective leaders. Often, this turned into getting top-level executive jobs.

What Ron was doing with exposure mentorship gave Black and Brown people the opportunity to get into a place where they could be seen. In the words of Ron, he did this "because they had great talent, yet were kind of hidden under a bush somewhere."

As I sat in my chair, pen in hand, I wrote down key points that came to mind:

1. Finding the right company who believes in your development is key.
2. Building genuine relationships with potential mentors.
3. Attend company events, engage in professional networks, and participate in activities that provide opportunities to connect with experienced professionals.
4. Do not limit yourself to a single mentor. Having multiple mentors with diverse experiences can provide a broader perspective and a richer learning experience.
5. Emphasize the value of being open to constructive comments. A mentorship relationship is a two-way street, and being open to assistance is essential for personal and professional success.

He continued. "They were being exposed in terms of being seen by people who make those kinds of decisions on who gets what. That was one way of exposing them."

He also believed corporations could model this for high school students. I thought to myself, *What would be the return of investment for them? I struggled with trying to sell this idea to organizations to take my students under their wings for mentorship...*

Ron, unprompted, had the answer to my question even though I hadn't asked it. It felt as though my thoughts were being projected for him to see.

"A person or organization seeking to connect young people to the world of work would have to sell the idea that they have very talented youth," Ron said.

I looked on with a touch of amazement as he continued his thought.

"The company that would host the scholars would first have to understand that the youth have a very limited view of what corporate life is like. By providing young people a day in the life at their company, they could plant a seed to inspire them to seek similar roles."

"Absolutely," I concurred. Hastily, I jotted down a brief thought to ensure it wouldn't slip my mind as I swiftly scribbled. I thought, *If this is done right, the relationship between company and student could turn the students into future employees once they were out of college.* This concept resembled my experience with career day but on a grander scale, catering to a substantial number of students. What if the company established a dedicated department, with a primary objective of crafting pathways for young individuals within the organization, thereby extending their commitment to the triple bottom line or forming a subsection within the DEI department?

It was a lightbulb moment.

As the interview neared its conclusion, Ron imparted a sense of hope to me. "The best of us don't get to where we are on our own. Someone somewhere helped."

Fortunately, certain organizations have already found solutions on how to establish pathways for today's generation.

After researching the mentoring effect, I took on the challenge of identifying an organization aligned with Ron's insights. My objective for the day was to participate in a workshop at the conference, aiming to connect with someone capable of pointing me in the right direction. With over a thousand attendees from fifty-six states and territories and twelve countries, and impressive seventy-four-person, in-person workshops, the day promised either a triumphant success or a redirection of my efforts.

Prior to the conference, we were given the task to register for our workshops. I felt a workshop that focused on partnerships may be the one to assist me on my quest on leveraging opportunities for my students. I gave myself five minutes. I thought, *If this is not what I need, I am going to sneak out back.*

I sat a few rows from the back and noticed the discussion was being led by a Black woman. Another Black woman and two white women were also part of the discussion. The presenter's name was Elycia Cook, chief executive officer at Big Brothers Big Sisters of Colorado, and she kicked us off with an interactive activity. Her voice commanded the room, and her presentation skills were similar to mine—high energy, interactive, and thought provoking. I was so caught up in the presentation I did not realize my five minutes were up. I stayed at the edge of my seat listening to her every word. It was truly a master class.

She explained to us the Pygmalion effect versus the Golem effect. According to the website The Decision Lab, "the *Pygmalion effect* describes situations where someone's high expectations improves our behavior and therefore our performance in a given area."[2] It implies when we are held to higher standards, we do better. The Golem effect, best described in an article in *Business Psychology* titled "Golem Effect vs. Pygmalion Effect," is a psychological phenomenon that is "the process where superiors (such as teachers or managers) anticipate low performance from a subordinate, causing the very behavior they predict."[3] This leads to poorer performance by the individual.

She showed us a slide on how we can move from equality to equity and liberation by giving those who have differences in height the appropriate box to stand on to see beyond the fence.

I leaned closer to the edge of my seat, knowing I was in the right place at the right time.

Finally, the moment I'd been waiting for arrived: Elycia presented on corporate partners in partnership with nonprofits. The slide title was named "Career Possibilities: Who Benefits," and it explained how corporate partners must support their talent gap, increase diversity, enhance employee engagement, and create a pipeline for the future workforce. Beneath that, it stated they were a nonprofit with their needs: mission focus and program enhancements, student engagement/workforce opportunities, new corporate revenue source/ROI, on-site employee engagement, and impactful corporate partnership.

Finally, her presentation zeroed in on youth, serving as the common thread that ties everything together. The youth require career exposure and exploration, networking opportunities across various industries, access to paid internships and scholarships, and the guidance of workforce mentors. Nonprofits and corporate partners can act as the bridge for our youth.

Everything in this slide was accurate and transformative. It was as if all the pieces of the puzzle were coming together and outlining how to build the next generation of diverse candidates for the workforce through exposure mentorship. Elycia introduced her partner organization BOA Technology, which creates technology that builds the scientifically proven and patented BOA Fit System.

Elissa Banker Brown, a resident in Colorado with a background in marketing and ten years of experience at BOA Technology, leads as the director of community development and partnerships. She stood up and introduced herself.

She spoke about the innovation of her company and the company's belief in their social responsibility. Her company, in partnership with Big Brothers Big Sister of Colorado, has a program called "Big Brothers Big Sisters Careers Possibilities Program," which is a paid internship that exposes youth from low-income and marginalized communities to career possibilities. In the promotion video, the CEO of company said, "It is really about career possibilities and life possibilities. It is exposing people, culture, ideas, jobs that these kids would have never ever seen."

Their partnership allows the littles, "also known as mentees," the opportunity to apply for this internship. If accepted, they receive $2,500 on the day of their graduation from the program.

I believe they figured out how to execute exposure mentorship in a way that can be modeled nationally. Although the concept is brilliant, the truth of it is not all companies have the right people in place to manage a program like this, especially for high school students. Was it the organization that was special in creating the opportunity for the interns, or was it the leaders who were in right position to make decision for a program such as this? It didn't take long for me to answer my question: both!

I knew at that moment I needed to interview both Elycia and Elissa to share their story on their partnership.

The presentation came to an end. I hurried to the front to obtain their business cards and asked if I could interview them. I knew nothing of their superhero origin stories. They had a passion for serving young people, and that was enough. They both agreed, and after interviewing them, I realized the strength of this partnership was rooted in having the right people in place who understood that with a more diverse workforce, ingenuity would increase.

After returning home from the conference, my head was spinning with so many thoughts. How could I replicate their success? If only I could have a partner like BOA Technology, which has caring, professional adults committed to serve as a "buddy" for each intern who enters the program and supports them while they are interning. I didn't waste any time and sent an email to both of them to coordinate the interview. My decision to reach out to Elissa first was a logical one. As the partner organization to Big Brothers Big Sisters, it made sense to hear her perspective on how this partnership came about and how they did not turn away from high school students as interns.

As the tips of my fingers pressed against the keyboard, I orchestrated a symphony of letters like a musician would on a piano.

> *Hi, Elissa. It was great meeting you during the mentor summit!*
>
> *This was my first time at the mentor summit, and I am feeling excited for the work that is ahead!*
>
> *It would be great to schedule a Zoom meeting with you to learn more about your work and share some of the things I am doing at Leaders of the 21st Century. Also, I*

am working on a book that will focus on mentorship and its impact on DEI. I believe you and BBBS are doing a great job. Would you be interested in being interviewed?

Please let me know when you might be available in the month of February or March.

Also, if you have the time and are looking for some inspiration, below you will find video links of some motivation and inspiration.

I look forward to hearing from you!

Best,
Dan

I clicked send with the expectation that a response would take a week. Knowing how busy people are, I was surprised she responded after only three days.

"I would be happy to set up a time to chat in any capacity. What does your schedule look like the week of February 27?" Elissa responded.

During my virtual interview with Elissa, I explained the difficulty as I'd seen it: "Many companies stir away from having high school students as interns, and if they have high school student interns, often times it's busy work."

With a nod, she responded, "It's not about work but about career possibilities."

So I asked about students who still struggled after completing internships.

But Elissa reassured me, "Our company trains the staff and matches the kids with a buddy."

We talked easily. Our conversation was relaxed and not rushed. Time flew by, and suddenly, we only had twenty minutes left of our hour together. I knew we would have to schedule another interview later because our talk deserved more time to delve deeper into things.

After I ended the meeting, I wrote myself a note on loose-leaf paper:

> *In the realm of leadership, the essence lies not in the person holding the role but in the service rendered to others. A genuine leader comprehends that they might not witness the fruition of the seeds they plant, the schools they construct, or the challenges they endure. Instead, they grasp the profound truth that future generations will reap the rewards of a sapling transformed into a sturdy tree, offering shade and bearing fruit.*

What set these two women apart? What endowed them with the unique understanding of this form of leadership, where the focus transcends personal gain to embrace a legacy of enduring impact?

FINAL LESSON

In the quest for personal and professional growth, you must strategically build and use your network. Choosing diverse and effective mentors carefully is key; they provide exposure and insights that help you move up in your career. Good mentors, who set high standards, play a vital role in your personal and professional development, influencing how you behave and perform.

The partnership between BOA Technology and Big Brothers Big Sisters is a great example of how collaborations between companies and nonprofits can bring lots of benefits. They focused on fixing talent gaps, making workplaces more diverse, keeping employees engaged, and preparing a strong workforce for the future. This shows how working together can make a big difference in addressing challenges related to diversity, equity, and inclusion.

Attending conferences and actively engaging with important people in those environments is a crucial part of personal development. This becomes even more effective when you focus on an area of interest that aligns with your goals. It's important to identify and nurture connections and support systems that match your ambitions.

CHAPTER 6

Mentorship: The Great Equalizer — Diversity, Equity, and Inclusion in Corporate Mentorship

When you think about Detroit, what first pops into your head? Is it the label "Motor City," reflecting its profound ties to the American automobile industry? Maybe you associate it with its musical heritage and pivotal role in genres like Motown and techno. You might also think about the tough economic times it went through, especially when it declared bankruptcy in the early 2010s. Alternatively, one might associate Detroit with legendary football running back Barry Sanders, who played for the Detroit Lions. In any case, perceptions of this city are diverse, and Detroit's narrative is intricate, marked by a blend of challenges and strengths that mold its identity.

"It's interesting because all of these shows about the mafia taking place out of Detroit—that was during my era," Elycia Cook expressed to me with eyes filled with purpose and pride.

I placed my right pointer finger in the middle of my glasses frame to slide them back up my nose as I listened to Elycia say this through the speakers of my laptop. Her expression remained neutral, like a poker player. But in this case, she was not bluffing. This was part of her story—the reality in which she grew up.

I was excited to reconnect and virtually interview Elycia. This interview would be the bridge in connecting great nonprofits to great corporate partnerships. I thought, *It is not common to see a Black woman as a CEO.*

In March 2021, Elycia became the first Black CEO of Big Brothers Big Sisters of Colorado, one of the largest youth mentoring organizations in the state. She spent twelve years as the president and CEO of FRIENDS FIRST, a peer-to-peer mentoring program for middle and high school students to discover and grow their own strengths and potential, developing their values and building health connections to lead a fulfilling life.

Before her success, it all started with her being a young girl growing up in one of the most challenging areas of Michigan, the city of Detroit. Born to a teen mother and father, Elycia became a first-generation high school graduate and college graduate.

With the guidance of mentors, she received a full scholarship to the Japan Center for Michigan Universities. She lived and worked in Japan for more than eight years and became fluent in speaking the language. She has taught Japanese to teens and, over the years, has helped young people visit, study, and live abroad.

We can all think of someone who made an impact in our lives that, if not for them, we would ask ourselves where we would be. For Elycia, it was a third-grade teacher who still supports her. Her teacher once said, "Girl, that gift of gab is going to make you money one day." Although Elycia would always get herself into trouble for talking, her teacher identified this as a strength and a skill that would separate her from her peers as a future leader.

This gift led to her being chosen as a youth newscaster, which her teacher made happen for her. This pinnacle moment started her on a trajectory where her "gift of gab" brought her to a very successful career. Her life is about storytelling and fundraising, influencing and negotiating, all of which started when her mentor exposed her to a career field she would otherwise have not had access to.

Years later, another mentoring encounter occurred. In tenth grade, another teacher took special interest in her. Elycia was a good student but also needed direction. Knowing she was born to teen parents, I can only imagine Elycia did not want to perpetuate the same generational cycle. She credits this teacher with helping her not make a choice that could have led her to becoming a teen mom.

In her *Los Angeles Times* article, "When Teen Pregnancy Runs in the Family," Martha Irvine writes, "The reasons behind the cycle of teen pregnancy are complicated and varied. But researchers do know that parents—present and absent—play a key role." Research indicates the disruption of education and employment opportunities for young mothers tends to sustain the cycle.

Elycia, a college student at the time, had a mentor who "literally plucked [her] out of the environment [she] was in and helped [her] to go study abroad." She was in Detroit at the time, and many people ended up in the auto industry, so it was no surprise for her to lean toward this path. She interned with General Motors and was scheduled to graduate the following year and planned to stay within a fifteen-mile radius of her house, but the dean of her business school had a different plan for this promising student.

College campuses are an oasis for building connections. Students can explore opportunities and discover who they are as a person. This is the best time to seek college internships and/or to work a part-time job. In Elycia's case, she decided to work in the dean's office of her business school. This led to her forming the relationship of mentee to her dean, Dr. Carpenter, who told her about an opportunity abroad in Japan.

But an important detail deterred Elycia. The program cost was twenty-six thousand dollars—money she did not have. But her mentor told her to apply, adding, "If you have the will, I will find the way."

Uncertain of the outcome and not fully convinced this was something she wanted to do, she applied because she had someone who believed in her. This is an attribute many of our youth could use. A little faith can motivate them to move mountains.

Elycia received her acceptance letter! Many people would jump with glee over this, but not Elycia. Rather than jumping and shouting, she tore it up, and said to herself, "That woman is crazy."

Fortunately, to Elycia's surprise, Dr. Carpenter also received the acceptance letter in the mail. She told Elycia, "We are going to Japan!" Elycia was awarded a scholarship but was still short fifteen thousand dollars. "I promised if you had the will, I'd find the way," her mentor reassured her. And like that, the two went on a campaign to raise the funds.

The mentor accompanied her to various churches, linked her up with the Black MBAs, all nine historically Black sororities and fraternities, and within three brief weeks, they gathered the funds. A month prior to departing for this esteemed opportunity, Elycia expressed to Dr. Carpenter she did not want to leave her family.

In the midst of Elycia recalling her journey, reminiscent of my own, the challenges of leaving family behind for educational pursuits echoed loudly.

As I listened to Elycia, I heard my own story in hers. At eleven, I had the opportunity to relocate and study— not abroad, but in a different state. She did not want to go, but I needed to leave because I would have ended up like others in my childhood neighborhood if I had not.

Dr. Carpenter understood her dilemma and what a life-changing opportunity this was for a young Black girl from Detroit. So, she did what great mentors would do: she listened.

After Dr. Carpenter heard Elycia's concerns, fears, and everything else holding her back, she said, "Before you make that decision, I want you to speak to one more person." Dr. Carpenter connected Elycia to the world-renowned Susan Taylor, who at the time was the editor-in-chief of *Essence Magazine*. She is an icon in the Black community who happened to be in Detroit for a speaking engagement.

"My sister, what is holding you back?" Susan said.

"My friends, family, my boyfriend," Elycia replied.

"Let me tell you something about people, especially those in your inner circle. They will be there when you get back if they are that important. But please don't hold yourself back from all that God is trying to offer and show you because you're afraid to leave your surroundings. My sister, go. My sister, go."

Elycia vows that someday this will be the title of the autobiography she dreams of writing someday.

As I continued to learn about Elycia's path from mentee to mentor, I asked her what her mentor taught her.

In that moment, she blinked twice and took a subtle pause as she collected her thoughts. "Well, it's true I went, I came back. And nobody was doing anything differently from what they were doing when I left. Yet I have been exposed to this whole world of opportunities, and that's literally defined my whole career, my whole trajectory, who I am.

"I sit here—you know, a Black woman in my fifties, fluent in Japanese, and a CEO of an organization who has helped many, many young people to go study abroad or have hosted many foreign exchange students. And quite frankly, a lot of those people were afraid to live. If they were still alive, they would be doing the same thing forty years later.

"I just wanted something different for my life. So, I really love talking to young people when they have a hard decision to make, especially if it plucks them out of their comfort zone or out of their environment. That's my kind of my platform for young people and particularly to go live abroad."

It made a lot of sense now as to why her presentation for the mentor summit was spoken with such an unwavering sense of conviction and passion. She was being the same sort of mentor she had all those years ago, guiding a whole new generation of people. She understood that unlocking doors demanded the benevolence of someone willing to entrust you with the key, enabling you to traverse and embrace what lay beyond.

What Elycia did is what other great mentors have done. She dissected her life and reflected on what worked, what didn't, and how to use this to become the best version of yourself. Her own journey of successes and obstacles became the driving force behind her decision to be a mentor. It's a deeply personal commitment that stems from within.

TRAGEDY AND TRIUMPHS

The same goes for Elissa, a New Jersey native who graduated from Syracuse University. In an unexpected twist, her professional journey veered off its anticipated course. Yet woven within the fabric of her narrative—a tapestry of tragedy and triumphs—laid the blueprint for a life brimming with positive outcomes. Through the avenues of mentorship and by exposing young minds to her field of work, she embarked on a compelling journey to contribute to making the world a better place.

Diagnosed with breast cancer at the age of thirty-one, she decided to launch her own nonprofit, Polite Tumor, which provides five-thousand-dollar grants to young adults in Colorado who have received the same diagnosis. She took a leap of faith in her career where passion met purpose, and where values, motivation, and skills would be aligned to a purpose driven position within her company. And just like that, she decided she wanted to go into corporate social responsibility where she now leads nonprofit partnerships, inclusion, and employee engagement.

Elissa, a white Jewish woman whose great-grandparents were immigrants, recognizes the privilege woven into her narrative and that each generation prior to her had to work harder. To Elissa, each successive generation appears to have had a more difficult time creating opportunities for the ones who followed. It's a legacy of perseverance, a continuous journey of providing what their predecessors could only dream of offering. Her circle of mentors started at an early age. Although she did not call them mentors at the time, her support system granted her access to pursue what she wanted as a career.

"I think about the privilege I had growing up. It was never a question whether or not I would have an internship," Elissa said with a self-aware tone. As she continued, I reflected on my students and how we are teaching them lessons in high school about internships, yet Elissa was exposed to this at a much earlier age. She said, "I had my parents being like, go find an internship. It wasn't an option, you know. It was what you did."

Elissa gets it and understands how some of us, despite how talented we may be or how great of grades we may have, will continue to fall by wayside without an exposure and mentorship pipeline of a diverse equitable inclusivity.

"How can kids create social capital they don't necessarily have access to? A network they already have in place because of where they live. Because they're from a low-income neighborhood and, like their parents, are not lawyers and doctors."

What Elissa said made sense. I knew she understood some doctors, lawyers, engineers, and those in other great professions still live in low-income neighborhoods. But I believe they are the minority who decided they do not want to move out yet stay within the community that raised them to assist with pushing the neighborhood forward. Nevertheless, those from low-income neighborhoods who are not as fortunate to climb out lack opportunities, which often repeats the cycle.

According to *NJ Spotlight News*, during the year 2022, the median household income in New Jersey for Blacks was $65,850 and $72,170 for Hispanics, while $106,209 for whites.[2]

"So how can we lessen the gap in terms of income inequality?" I asked.

"Being able to provide these kids with social capital from an early age—like fifteen, sixteen, seventeen—is what's going to launch them into that next echelon of education or into the workforce," Elissa responded.

Everything Elissa does for her company is connected to diversity, equity, and inclusion, so it made sense why this partnership between Big Brothers Big Sisters of Colorado and BOA Technology would exist and that both female minority leaders would lead this amazing endeavor of providing an opportunity of a lifetime. Exposing kids to BOA Technology career pathways is part of the company's inclusion roadmap and part of their community plan. They seek to ensure they are diversifying not only their business, but the industry as a whole.

Elissa believes this partnership that allows BBBS Colorado mentees to apply for an internship within BOA Technology is not intended to keep them working for BOA Technology after their internship, and that's okay. The point is that you've exposed somebody else who wouldn't necessarily have exposure to that work and broadened their view of what's possible. "So, I do think it's important for it to be part of a diversity, equity, and inclusion strategy, but I also think it's important for it to be embedded within other areas of the company," Elissa said with a warm smile.

Both women were born in different communities, one in a large urban city versus the suburbs of New Jersey. One was born white and as a descendant of immigrants, while the other was born Black to two teen parents. In one story, you can see how privilege played a role in her success, which she acknowledges. The other paints a story of a community where aspirations vary depending on the circumstances of the individual.

Both women graduated from high school and college, but the great equalizer was not education. Education may have separated them from their peers, but what connects both stories is the mentorship they received throughout their lives. One set of mentors were already established based on access from birth while the other set of mentors were established by relationships along the journey.

Education did allow Elycia access to resources she would not have had if it was not for graduating from high school and college, and it was education that allowed Elissa access to her first job. But the constant variable in both their stories, which led them to serve in the capacity of building a diverse next generation of career-ready leaders, was the exposure they received and mentors they gained.

FINAL THOUGHTS

What season are you in that your mentor can be here for? What is the area of impact in which you need guidance?

In essence, the profound impact of mentorship in navigating life's complexities is that it unlocks doors to unforeseen possibilities and fosters a commitment to uplift the next generation. The stories of Elycia and Elissa exemplify the transformative power of mentorship, transcending backgrounds and challenges, and illuminating a path toward personal and professional fulfillment.

Despite different backgrounds and privileges, what connects Elycia and Elissa is the constant variable of mentorship throughout their lives. Mentorship emerges as the great equalizer in building a diverse next generation of career-ready leaders.

Elissa's story introduces the concept of privilege and how early exposure and mentorship played a crucial role in her career. The discussion on income inequality and the importance of providing social capital underscores the significance of mentorship in leveling the playing field.

Elycia's journey, from mentee to mentor, showcases the ripple effect of mentorship. Her commitment to guiding a new generation highlights the cyclical nature of positive influence and the responsibility of those mentored to pay it forward.

Educational opportunities play a huge role shaping one's future. Elycia's mentor facilitated her study abroad opportunity, demonstrating how education can open doors to a world of opportunities. Her upbringing in challenging circumstances in Detroit, coupled with mentorship, allowed her to become a first-generation high school and college graduate, illustrating the power of resilience and guidance.

Supportive teachers as mentors, especially Elycia's third-grade teacher, tenth-grade teacher, and college dean, played crucial roles as mentors. They identified her strengths, guiding her away from potential pitfalls and ultimately influencing her trajectory. Their faith and belief in her motivated her to overcome obstacles.

The partnership between Big Brothers Big Sisters of Colorado and BOA Technology exemplifies the importance of diversity, equity, and inclusion strategies in corporate initiatives. This partnership is a tangible example of how corporate initiatives can be designed to go beyond traditional business goals and actively contribute to societal advancement by fostering diversity, equity, and inclusion. It aligns with broader social and corporate responsibility principles, creating a positive impact on individuals, communities, and the industry as a whole.

CHAPTER 7

Cultivating Connections: The Transformative Power of Mentorship and Networking

Amid the ever-changing waves of the working world, one immovable truth reigns supreme: mentorship has transformative power. Mentoring expands the mentor-mentee portfolio. The ability to accept lifelong learning provides a considerable advantage. The mentor-mentee relationship should extend beyond the immediate professional context and include networking and relationship-building. Networking not only opens new opportunities, but it also exposes mentors and mentees to a variety of perspectives. A strong professional network forms an important part of the mentor-mentee portfolio, allowing career progression and success.

I recently read 70 percent of jobs are not posted online. Therefore, the relationships one builds are key to climbing the ladder in their career. This comes with the hope that they too will mentor and guide someone else on how to navigate the professional landscape of becoming employed. Networking is a critical skill to learn if you want to advance in your career. It is defined by Columbia University Center for Career Education as the process of making connections and building relationships.[1]

A person's network and contacts can frequently have a substantial impact on finding work. The cliché "it's not just what you know, but who you know" is valid, since networking is essential in job search. Personal contacts, referrals, and recommendations can give candidates a competitive advantage in a congested employment market. Building and maintaining a strong professional network can lead to unexpected opportunities, help with job advancement, and improve overall professional performance. As a result, in addition to polishing skills and qualifications, people are increasingly realizing the need of developing meaningful relationships to negotiate the complexity of the job market.

Many years ago, I realized the importance of this lesson. Without my network, I would not have had the opportunity to travel to South Africa, pursue fellowship programs, or receive my master's degree. My mentors and the networking possibilities they provided played a critical role in shaping my life. However, it is important to recognize not all networking experiences begin well.

The sun was still out as I walked toward my car parked in front of the building. I had plans later that evening to finish up the list of the community members who would come into the school during the day and read a book to our students. The students were not proficient in reading and far beyond the mark to reach grade level.

However, the Children's Defense Fund Freedom Schools program had the ability to change that through their model. My team and I had witnessed significant growth in our students during the four weeks. It was a disheartening experience on the first day, seeing young Black and Brown kids entering the program with low literacy levels. By the end of the week, I noticed a remarkable transformative increase in their reading levels.

Freedom Schools empowers students to believe in their ability and responsibility to make a difference while instilling in them a love of reading to help them avoid summer learning loss. The program provides summer and after-school enrichment through a research-based and multicultural program model that supports K–12 scholars and their families through five essential components:

High quality academic and character-building enrichment.

- Parent and family involvement.
- Civic engagement and social action.
- Intergenerational servant leadership development.
- Nutrition, health, and mental health.[2]

"See you tomorrow," I shouted through the double doors in the front of the school building as I made my way to my red Honda Accord. I opened my car door and noticed my middle console was open and the items inside laid scattered across the passenger seat. I took a pause and thought, *When did I open this, and what did I grab from here?* It had been a long day, so I blamed this on a memory lapse. The car key would not go in. I tried again, and this time I looked and noticed the key ignition was popped out. I realized someone had broken in and attempted to steal my car. In disbelief, I sat in my car for a couple of minutes before I called the police.

This was my city, and a break-in did not deter me from coming into work the next day. I knew when I took the role something like this could occur. Although I did not think it could happen during the day in front of a school, I was reminded that desperation makes anything possible. And my presence in these kids' lives was more important than my car. At the time, I was a graduate student working on my master's degree in public administration and understood my life mission was to serve and make this world a better place through love, service, and faith.

It was 2015, my first summer of graduate school. I was working as the project director for Rutgers Newark Freedom School, held in one of the local elementary schools in Newark. In my role, I coordinated all the operational logistics with the executive director, Dr. John Johnson. My team included Dr. Joanna Maulbeck, who led over the summer curriculum and four college students in the role of site coordinators.

Each morning, we started the day with "*harambee*," which is a Swahili word that means "let's pull together." From cheers and chants to recognizing students in the program and singing the motivational song "Something Inside So Strong" by Labi Siffre, the hallways were filled with children voices singing with such passion, pain, and hope.

Later that summer, as we came to the end of the program, Kyle Farmbry, dean of Rutgers University, Newark Graduate School, came with his team for a visit to see us in action. He helped secure funding for Freedom School. Our conversation was brief, but the few words we shared served as a seed that would blossom into a mentor-mentee relationship.

As I entered my final year of graduate school, it was important for me to build relationships with my professors and my classmates. I had two goals: to graduate with honors and to develop networking skills. Whether it was coffee with a professor or happy hour with classmates, I wanted to ensure I did not just attend graduate school for a master's degree but to also leave with lasting friendships. This was part of the reason I took a leap of faith and left my job to attend graduate school as a full-time student. If the school had a social gathering for the students, I attended. If a professor had a job opportunity that aligned with my interests, I applied. I was determined to leave the campus better than how I found it, as an effective leader and student.

During my final year, I was in a grant writing class. My major was nonprofit management, and grant writing was a fundamental requirement to graduate. My grant writing professor was going over a few things while I checked my school email. I was not in the habit of checking this account since I always gave out my personal email to my classmates and staff members on campus, but for some reason I checked.

Maybe it was fate or simply the fact that my professor had lost my attention. Either way, all I saw were hundreds of emails marked unread, but I was drawn to one in particular. It read, "Innovation Alliance for Social Enterprise Development Fellowship."

The email detailed how this fellowship was a grant from the United States Agency for International Development (USAID), in partnership with the Rutgers Center for Global Advancement and International Affairs (GAIA), as part of its Global Fellowship Program. I had no clue what USAID was, and I'd never even heard of GAIA, but I was interested in learning more. I knew if I could get a hold of someone in the department maybe they could answer some of my questions.

As I continued to read the description, I recognized the name of the faculty member who oversaw this initiative for Rutgers University: Dean Kyle Farmbry. My eyes lit up with surprise and excitement. I could not believe I knew him. I could no longer hear the voice of my professor, only my thoughts: *Wow, this looks like this could be an awesome opportunity. I wonder what the requirements are to participate.* I did something I learned during my previous professional roles. I sent a well-drafted professional email over to Dr. Farmbry telling him I was interested and to ask if he was looking for anything in particular in a qualified candidate.

He responded within minutes, saying the deadline to apply was that night and asking if I could turn the application around in time.

Without reading through the application, I responded with certainty: "Yes."

For a tantalizing few weeks after applying, I waited. Then, one day, the email popped up: my application was approved. Receiving this confirmation, I felt relieved. Alongside six others, I was accepted from an extremely competitive application pool to embark on a mission to make a difference in South Africa.

During the two-month fellowship, we collaborated with the Community Chest of the Western Cape, a South African organization devoted to social change and community development. Founded in 1928, the Community Chest engages in public and private partnerships to strengthen South African communities through increased access to health, education, and employment opportunities. Upon our arrival, the Community Chest offered us guidance as we integrated with the community, traveled to schools and local centers for interviews, and shared in the lives and experiences of locals while gathering data.

It was our version of United Way, which seeks to improve lives by mobilizing the caring power of communities around the world to advance the common good.[3]

We worked with Community Chest representatives prior to our arrival to develop projects that matched our research interests with areas of need in Cape Town. My research was to analyze the strengths and shortcomings in the existing STEM education curriculum and find ways to enhance STEM education for children in economically disadvantaged areas. I wanted to have an impact on the people.

We had the goal of changing this community. But the first week, I began to understand the impact was the other way around. They all impacted me. If I could measure what I was doing for them, it wouldn't even compare to what they had done for me.

During my free time, I wandered the streets, striking up conversations with strangers and making connections I could not have imagined. People shared stories of poverty, community, and memories of the brutality endured under South Africa's apartheid government. My friendly approach and understanding of networking led to an invitation from a local disc jockey to attend a traditional circumcision ceremony and a chance encounter with a One Republic band member who gave me VIP tickets to their Cape Town concert.

Not every student had the same good fortune of forging bonds so easily. I did because I had the ability to network. My role as the director of the Freedom Schools served as an audition and led to this opportunity for the USAID fellowship. If it was not for the effective work at Freedom Schools, I do not think my application would have been considered. I was qualified for the opportunity; however, the relationship with Dr. Farmbry allowed me the privilege to email him and receive clarity on the application process.

So it was no surprise when I logged into my social media account and read that Guilford College had selected Dr. Farmbry as their new college president. From dean to college president, he was a man who dedicated himself to higher education and spent a good amount of time helping young adults obtain their doctorate. But like all great leaders and effective mentors, their story of why they enter their career field is always the reflection of someone who exposed them to it.

President Farmbry grew up watching his uncle, who was a professor. "Over time, I got to see this really wonderful field where people's careers were really focused on touching the lives of students. As I started to go further along and, somehow, I ended up where I am." One would think somehow his commitment to academic excellence happened by happenstance, but during his interview he spoke about how some great people provided lots of insight and opportunities to him at different stages.

The *Journal of Blacks in Higher Education* reported the American Council on Education found the college presidency remains older, white, and male. The report found in 2022, 77.2 percent of college and university presidents were white. Blacks or African Americans made up 13.6 percent of college or university presidents, approximately equal to the percentage of Blacks in the US population. Furthermore, Blacks made up 14.1 percent of all women college or university presidents and 13.3 percent of all male presidents.[4]

President Farmbry was not asked why the numbers were so low, but based on his interview it was clear his position in leadership serves as an example of creating opportunities for all students but also for professors of color. Guilford College roughly serves 50 percent students of color, yet only 3 percent of the professors are of color, which leads President Farmbry with a brilliant initiative regarding his intentional leadership to support diversity, equity, and inclusion by making sure he brings faculty who reflect the student body.

As I continued to listen to President Farmbry, I thought about how much representation matters especially when historically many people of color were not granted a seat at the table, let alone the ability to enter the room. Although we have made tremendous strides compared to one hundred years ago, work remains that needs to allow those who have been barred from financial freedom and the chance to work in positions we were not granted access to work in previously.

He embarked on creating what he calls "dissertation bootcamp," which allows people working on their dissertations to come together and focus their time. After I let this sink in, I asked why. He replied, "Part of my reason for doing that is because I need to build a pipeline into faculty roles here and elsewhere."

I typically try not to interject my thoughts during the interview, but I could not help myself. "That's genius! Very innovative."

Because President Farmbry was indirectly exposed by his uncle to higher education, he understood junior high or high school students should have an idea of a career. However, a disparity issue remains. He said, "Some kids see mom and dad or uncle or aunt who's a lawyer or a doctor or a businessperson, and others don't because they just don't come from those backgrounds." I thought of my own story and how limited my exposure was to certain professions as a young kid. But when I moved to Geneva, I was surrounded by industries and people in careers I never knew existed.

President Farmbry continued. "So, for the kid who sees mom or dad or uncle or aunt who's a lawyer or a doctor, they have a sort of informal exposure, mentorship that takes place. So if we can particularly supplement those opportunities for kids who don't, then that's great and overall a good thing."

Kyle is a mentor to many and truly an inspiration to me. He is humble and grateful for those who came before him. Out of curiosity, I asked him if those in positions of mentoring and exposing others to their careers should know anything, mainly because I think great mentorship can be replicated. His response was this: "It's important to think about where you came from and all the people who guided you along the way. And, you know, I don't think anyone—if you're in a real role of importance, however you want to define that—gets there alone. And I think that's easily forgotten. I think it's important for people to think about their paths and how others have supported them over the years."

I took great pride in interviewing Kyle. Like many others who were mentored by him at various stages of his life, my encounter with him occurred when I was a young graduate student navigating the complexities of life. Kyle ensured I had exposure by involving me in his office on special projects. It was through him that I first delved into the realm of social entrepreneurship and set up my initial trading investment account.

During a conversation about investing, I confessed I hadn't started due to limited funds and the burden of student loans. He encouraged me, emphasizing the key was to begin, regardless of the amount. His mentorship extended to special events where I represented Rutgers Graduate School. Given my major in nonprofit management and my background in grant writing, Kyle invited me to collaborate with him and another professor on a grant proposal. Despite doubts from the other professor, I reassured her we would succeed, and indeed, we secured the grant. These experiences with Kyle significantly bolstered my confidence and underscored the vital importance of cultivating a strong professional network.

THE POWER OF NETWORKING IN EIGHT STEPS

Within our curriculum of Leaders of the 21st Century, we explain to our students how powerful the skill of networking is and how it is important to use your network to identity yourself a mentor. Rather than creating an asset map which provides information about the strengths and resources a community has in order to discover the solutions for the community, our students are given the task to create a social capital map. This allows them to identify those within their current network, and they wish to have someone in their network they can create a wish list.

This principle of networking should be taught to college students, entry level professionals, and senior level professionals. It would allow those who seek to gain an upper hand within their career the opportunity to do so. Some, like President Farmbry mentioned, were informally exposed to a network of people. These individuals did not need to network to gain access to their career due to the fact that they grew up in their circle of influence.

The hope is you too are able to grow and expand your circle of influence. I believe one must take fundamental steps to build genuine relationships regarding networking and seeking mentorships. It involves a combination of authenticity, mutual value, and effective communication.

Here are eight steps to help you build meaningful connections through networking:

- Clarify your goals: Specify your objectives for networking. Identify your goals, whether they involve growing your professional network, finding a mentor, or learning about the sector.

  - Benefit: clearly defined goals provide direction in networking efforts.
  - Outcome: helps individuals focus on specific objectives, whether it's expanding their professional network, finding a mentor, or gaining sector knowledge.

- Identify target contacts: Find others who share your objectives. This could be coworkers, industry peers, or experts in your field of interest.

  - Benefit: identifying contacts with shared objectives enhances the relevance of the network.
  - Outcome: increases the likelihood of meaningful connections with individuals who align with one's professional goals.

- Research: Get to know the individuals you wish to interact with. Recognize their hobbies, occupation, and any shared interests.

  - Benefit: researching individuals beforehand allows for informed and meaningful interactions.
  - Outcome: establishes a foundation for conversations, making them more engaging and demonstrating genuine interest.

- Build an online professional presence: Establish a professional online identity on sites such as LinkedIn. Join industry groups, participate in discussions, and share pertinent content.

  - Benefit: building an online presence enhances visibility and credibility.
  - Outcome: facilitates connections beyond physical boundaries, attracting like-minded professionals and opportunities.

- Attend networking events: Participate in networking events, workshops, and conferences that can result in more sincere relationships and possible leads to jobs.
    - Benefit: actively participating in networking events provides opportunities for in-person communication.
    - Outcome: allows for more personal and sincere relationships, creating a stronger network and potential job leads.
- Initiate conversations: Strike up a genuine conversation. Engage in active listening, ask open-ended inquiries, and share your interests with others.
    - Benefit: initiating genuine conversations with active listening fosters stronger connections.
    - Outcome: establishes rapport and trust, making interactions more meaningful and increasing the likelihood of long-term professional relationships.
- Provide value: Offer support or pertinent information. Assisting people fosters reciprocity and trust in professional relationships.
    - Benefit: providing value to others creates a culture of reciprocity.
    - Outcome: builds trust within the network, leading to more collaborative opportunities and support from others.
- Continued relationship building: Follow up by sending a personalized email to convey your interest in carrying on the conversation after an event or first meeting
    - Benefit: following up with personalized emails demonstrates ongoing interest and commitment.
    - Outcome: strengthens connections over time, turning initial interactions into lasting professional relationships.

Following these steps will bring you closer to increasing your network to a different level. All of what is mentioned are the steps I use when building my own network. It requires you to step outside your comfort zone, but just like a muscle, you must exercise these steps. After a while of practice, this will become second nature as part of your professionalism as a leader. This has separated me from my peers, and I am sure it will do the same for you.

FINAL LESSONS

The transformative impact of education, mentorship, and networking are three of the key themes within this chapter. Despite encountering challenges—such as a car break-in—it is crucial for you to maintain an unwavering commitment, showcasing your resilience required to pursue your broader mission.

Mentors play a pivotal role in shaping your career opportunities. The mentor-mentee relationship typically starts as a planted seed, eventually blossoming into valuable connections that lead to more significant and enriching experiences. This, in turn, becomes an integral part of your learning journey. The ability to network effectively is a crucial skill that opens doors to various opportunities and collaborations, exemplified by engagements like the USAID fellowship and participation with the Community Chest in Cape Town.

Also, a professional mentor/mentee relationship may evolve into a more personal one, and that's perfectly acceptable. Welcoming such shifts adds depth to the connection.

Networking is powerful, and the significance of intentional relationships is crucial to your career advancement. Having a mentor advocate for you and imparting networking skills can set you apart from the rest.

The eight steps emphasize the importance of setting goals, identifying target contacts, researching, building an online presence, attending events, initiating conversations, providing value, and following up. Through these steps, cultivating connections is a transformative method to the broader message about the interconnectedness of education, mentorship, and networking. In navigating your professional journey, you can and will create opportunities for personal and collective growth.

CHAPTER 8

Navigating Spaces with Authenticity: Trusting Your Brilliance

Knowing yourself before asking for assistance can help you navigate spaces with authenticity. What's your own image?

Have you ever envied someone so much you wanted to be just like them? That's the tactic Gatorade used in 1992 when it produced what is arguably known as Michael Jordan's most well-known commercial, titled "Be Like Mike." The advertisement featured numerous highlights from Jordan's NBA career as well as scenes of him interacting with children. In the ad, he dribbled, jumped, and shot the ball, and the youngsters emulated what they saw, including how he famously stuck out his tongue while making a layup. The goal of the video was to get viewers to follow Michael Jordan's example and consume Gatorade because of his powerful personal brand and the fact that many others aspired to be like him.

I said, "Good morning, everyone," and grinned broadly at the students. "Today's workshop will concentrate on branding and marketing yourself." I showed them a variety of logos, including those for Pizza Hut, Apple, McDonald's, etc. and asked which they liked most. The students were really involved and spoke openly about whatever logo appealed to them.

Some students chuckled when one student yelled, "Gucci!" Gucci was not on the list when I looked at the samples I had posted, but I did not mind because I knew by calling his preferred brand, he would help reinforce the lesson intended for the day.

They had to respond to a few questions as part of their assignment. I asked, "What do you think of and how do you feel when you see this Amazon Prime logo?"

Students said excitement, hunger, and even holiday shopping. I gave them the assignment to find a brand that shares their fundamental beliefs and values. "It could be a person or a business, but either way, when you are finished, you will come forward and present," I stated to the class as they signed into their desktops to type out their responses.

I selected a student and asked, "Who or what did you choose?"

"My mother," she replied. "My mom is inspired by her children to become the best she can be in this world, and she doesn't have a single selfish bone in her body. I am trying my best to be like that."

I cheered her on and encouraged the class to do the same. Other students chose Steve Jobs while another chose Rihanna.

The point of this exercise was to examine other brands that exist in the world and think of themselves as a brand. What do you want others to think when they hear your name? In the previous chapter, I mentioned it is not who you know but also who knows you, and I also explained the importance of cultivating connections. The person who will speak on behalf of you, what will they say about you? I made sure to explain that finding a right mentor to model could help shape your brand.

Branding yourself is crucial because it reflects who you are. It involves creating a distinct and authentic identity that represents your unique qualities, values, expertise, and reputation. It can help you distinguish yourself, enhance your professional opportunities, and establish credibility. Creating your own brand is a continuous process that evolves over time. You must be patient, stay focused, and consistently invest in building and nurturing your personal brand. With dedication and authenticity, you can establish a strong report that distinguishes you and opens doors to new opportunities.

Kalina Bryant, *Forbes* 30 under 30

The person who can help point you in the right direction so your resume stands out is a mentor willing and able to connect you with other professionals who have gained success throughout their career.

If the mentor does not believe you are qualified to connect with individuals in their network, they will not make the connection on your behalf. It is critical to understand just like all the other big brands you must carry yourself with the same integrity they do.

Throughout my interview process, I wanted to interview a *Forbes* 30 under 30 trailblazer, but I faced a challenge. I did not know anyone who had achieved that level of recognition. So, I did what most people do in the twenty-first century: I did my research, and on January 30, 2023, at 7:44 p.m., I sent a direct message to Kalina Bryant on Instagram:

"Hi Kalina, my name is Dan De Nose from Newark, New Jersey, who is currently on a quest/process of writing a book focusing on mentorship and its impact on DEI within companies. I am the CEO/founder of a nonprofit in my city working with youth to develop their leadership/professional development skills for life after high school. I am reaching out to those who I believe can help define DEI through the lens of mentorship and would be honored to interview you. Would it be possible to coordinate and interview within the month of February or March? I would be honored! If there is anything that you need from me to make this possible, please let me know. Thank you and I look forward to hearing from you."

I prepared myself to not receive a response, but she quickly answered: "Hey! Thanks for your note. Happy to help where I can. Send me an email at…"

Kalina Bryant's resume of accomplishments is impressive: she was the first African American woman to join Asana's revenue executive leadership team and pioneered the Employee Resource Group for Black employees at the company. Her skill set and level of expertise helped bring in nine million dollars in annual revenue for the company.

When Kalina said yes to the interview, I felt like I'd won the lotto. I was beyond excited and thankful because I knew her perspective as someone on the *Forbes* 30 under 30 list would give me valuable insight.

During her interview, a common theme resonated throughout our conversation around her brand. Who she was as a human being allowed others to make room for her in spaces that often were not made available to Black women. Her experiences, whether being denied employment or getting her dream job, all shaped her personal and professional brand.

I knew very little of Kalina's personal story. My research online gave me in-depth information regarding her professional journey. Like all successful entrepreneurs, her personal story acted as a catalyst to her entering the tech world.

"What made you go into your field of work?" I asked. She tilted her head down, and her hair bun resembled a queen's crown. She paused, then answered my question. Through the glasses on her face, I saw her eyes in a focused gaze as she told me her story.

In 2014, Kalina graduated from St. Mary's College in California. She was born and raised in California and lived only twenty-five minutes away from Beverly Hills. "I was exposed to a lot of individuals, executives in the tech industry," Kalina said.

Kalina told me about her college years, how she'd babysit for up to four families at a time to help pay for her to study abroad in London and the Dominican Republic. It just so happened the year she was to graduate, one of her babysitting gigs ended up being for a gentleman whose girlfriend was vice president of sales for a tech company. He knew Kalina was a hard-working student and she was serious about her studies.

As I listened to Kalina, I realized part of her brand was her appreciation for education, perseverance, strong work ethic, and compassion. Branding often aligns with your morals and values.

Kalina looked at me, her gaze distant, then recounted, "He asked what my plans were after graduation, and I replied, 'I should go to graduate school, but I think I need to work a little bit and get some things under my belt.' He said, 'I will talk to my girlfriend when she and I go out to dinner.'"

Before the gentlemen and his girlfriend went to dinner, the girlfriend provided Kalina with her business card.

Kalina recounted that meeting. "They returned from dinner, and the girlfriend said, 'You call me. You know... If you want a job.'"

Kalina had no idea what enterprise technology was, so, only a month after graduating from college, she applied as an intern for a top PR firm. To her surprise she was not accepted. Discouraged and desperate, she finally called the gentleman's girlfriend. She interviewed for a role with Marketa and got the job.

Now a decade later, she can tell you what an IPO versus a pre-IPO is, she is a *Forbes* 30 under 30 honoree and editorial contributor, marketing and customer growth executive, podcast host, advisor, and a speaker. She is the founder and head of marketing for UnapologeTECH, which is a professional training and coaching firm dedicated to bettering corporations and building up diverse talent.

Kalina said, "Being the only person of color, especially a Black woman in that field, you know, you can either cry and say, 'Hey, this is not fair, and I don't fit in.' Or you can get to a point where you understand that numbers don't lie, and numbers have no color. So, I went that route. I started understanding how to work with these companies, how to pivot, how to pitch, and that led me into understanding how to pick companies."

Kalina did not come from a wealthy family, but her family decided to pay for her education. They equipped her to access all the education they could and everything they knew, and it was up to her to make it work. She took advantage of the opportunity she was given in the tech world, which allowed her to become a *Forbes* 30 under 30 honoree on her third IPO and building out her own organization. She, like many talented women, only needed the right exposure, but she had also been building a brand during her most formidable years.

STEPS TO BRAND YOURSELF

Eight steps have been extremely helpful in branding myself throughout my career.

Step 1. Define your brand identity: Start by defining who you are, what you stand for, and what sets you apart from others. Identify your values, passions, strengths, and areas of expertise. Consider your unique skills, experiences, and personal qualities that make you stand out.

Step 2. Understand your target audience: Determine who your target audience is and what they value. This could be employers, clients, industry peers, or a specific community. Understand their needs, preferences, and areas of struggle to align your brand with their expectations and interests.

Step 3. Craft your brand message: Develop a clear and concise brand message that communicates your unique value proposition. It should effectively convey who you are, what you offer, and why others should pay attention to you. This message should be consistent across your communication channels.

Step 4. Establish an online presence: In today's digital age, having a strong online presence is crucial. Create a professional website or portfolio that showcases your expertise, accomplishments, and personal brand. Utilize social media platforms, such as LinkedIn, to build your professional network, share valuable content, and engage with your target audience.

Step 5. Network and build relationships: Actively engage in networking activities to connect with industry professionals, thought leaders, and potential collaborators. Attend events, join professional associations, and participate in online communities. Building genuine relationships can expand your reach and open doors for new opportunities.

Step 6. Showcase your expertise: Position yourself as an expert in your field by sharing your knowledge and insights. Speak at conferences or industry events, blog posts or offer to be a guest on relevant podcasts. Establishing yourself as a thought leader helps to build credibility and visibility.

Step 7. Seek feedback and adapt: Regularly seek feedback from trusted mentors, colleagues, or clients to gauge how your personal brand is perceived. Adjust and refine your brand strategy as needed to ensure it remains relevant, authentic, and aligned with your goals.

Step 8. Maintain authenticity: Authenticity is key to building a strong personal brand. Be true to yourself, showcase your unique personality, and let your values guide your actions. Building trust and credibility requires consistency between your brand identity and your actual behavior.

PERSONALIZE YOUR BRAND

As a founder, executive director, social entrepreneur, and motivational speaker in the business of assisting others in becoming their best selves, I have found most individuals have already established a social media brand for themselves. Whatever we put out into the world, whether it be personally or professionally, reveals who we are. You get to determine what information about yourself that you want the world to know, but more crucially, what information you do not want the world to know.

There is a saying: "Not everything is for everyone." Some things are meant for just you and your family, and some things are meant for just your friends. You have the power to code-switch, which is defined by Dictionary.com as "the modifying of one's speech, behavior, appearance, etc. to adapt to different sociocultural norms."[1] You can select which version of yourself is suited for your audience.

I discovered a vital lesson while working in the human resources division: recruiting managers conduct their homework before interviews. It is not a question of whether people will Google you, but rather, what they find when they do. I assigned this project with my students, and many of them were startled by what they found themselves tagged and/or mentioned in or because their name appeared in an article a long time ago after winning a track championship. Everyone has a digital footprint, so it is important for the mentee to understand how to brand themselves in order to gain employment.

Building your mentor team and developing your personal brand are related concepts. Being exposed to excellent examples to emulate will help improve any facet of one's image, especially if you are trying to reinvent yourself or fine tune any abilities you are having trouble with. When "Be Like Mike" first aired, it was more than just an ad for kids; it was a guide for what to aim for. You must be who you are, yet mentors have discovered things that can guide you in the right direction.

Both having a mentor and building a personal brand contribute significantly to your professional success and satisfaction. A mentor provides guidance and support, while a strong personal brand enhances your visibility, credibility, and career opportunities. Together, they create a powerful combination for a successful and fulfilling professional journey.

FINAL LESSONS

The Gatorade commercial featuring Jordan serves as a compelling illustration of how modeling success can propel you forward, providing a solid foundation for grasping the intricacies of building your personal branding.

As you delve into the importance of your personal brand, it's crucial to adopt a strategic mindset regarding the impressions you make on others. Pay close attention to the role mentorship plays in shaping your brand; it's a key factor in your professional development.

Let's turn our attention to Kalina's journey, a narrative punctuated by unwavering perseverance, a commitment to education, and a brand alignment with personal values. Her story stands as an inspiring case study, urging you to embark on the journey of defining your own personal brand.

Now, let's explore the eight steps for effective personal branding, underlining the ongoing evolution of your brand. Concepts like personalization, code-switching, and managing your digital footprint emphasize the paramount importance of authenticity throughout your branding process. Understand the intricate dance between mentorship and personal branding, recognizing their combined impact on your professional success and overall fulfillment.

Branding yourself is important for several reasons, particularly in the professional and personal realms. Strong personal brand gives you influence and allows you to make a positive impact. Whether in your workplace or your community, people are more likely to listen to and follow individuals with a well-established personal brand. Personal branding is a strategic tool that empowers you to control how others perceive you. It is a dynamic process that evolves over time and requires continuous investment, but the benefits can be substantial in terms of career success, networking, and personal fulfillment.

In essence, personal branding serves as a tool for self-discovery, self-expression, and intentional living. When individuals actively shape their personal brand to reflect their true selves, it creates a pathway to fulfillment by fostering authenticity, purpose, meaningful connections, and continuous growth.

This may take time and will be a lifelong journey, but to know yourself and to be true to who you are is an amazing feeling as a professional. You must lead with integrity and stand on your values. Just like a company who stands on their values, you must do the same: think of yourself as your own business entity.

Remember, as you navigate different spaces, authenticity should be your guiding principle. Your greatest strength lies in being the remarkable individual you are. Allow your brilliance to shine brightly, revealing your true self to the world. Trust the right mentor will emerge as you diligently build your brand.

CHAPTER 9

Beyond the Podium: The Power of Mentorship in Public Speaking

What age were you when you met someone who truly believed in you? Sometimes all it takes for a young person to believe in themselves is to have a caring adult who tells them, "You can do it! I believe in you! No matter what, I still love you. Nothing is impossible if you have a positive mindset, hard work, and the belief to never give up. That you become what you think. If you believe you are great, you will be great. You are destined for great things in this world. You are uniquely created to do amazing things, and because of you the world will be a better place."

This type of outpouring of unconditional love and sometimes even tough love prepares our youth to enter the world with confidence that includes perseverance, grit, and ambition. The statement you are what you think reflects the idea that our thoughts and beliefs play a significant role in shaping our identity, behavior, and overall well-being.

A positive mindset can lead to positive outcomes and better life experiences. Granted, many external factors and other influences are in conjunction with this adage. Nevertheless, if you believe it, you can achieve it. This is half the battle when assisting in developing our young leaders for college, career, or trade—especially those who come from a background where they lack hope due to their environment and lack of opportunities.

On May 13, 2023, my NGO Leaders of the 21st Century graduated its fifth batch of seniors. The students must meet specific standards to graduate from the program. They are required to attend our Saturday sessions. They participate in planning the service project initiatives we conduct for homeless families, as well as the spring symposium. Finally, they must prepare a five-minute graduation speech and present it during their graduation. Because many of our young people lack the public speaking experience, we give them three sessions that focus on rhetoric, teaching them how to compose and develop a speech.

I teach them everything I know about rhetoric. During my time at Hobart and William Smith, I developed my own major, Rhetoric of Leadership. I studied and investigated the talent of being a great orator, as well as the five canons of rhetoric required to construct a great speech.

The five canons of rhetoric are:

- Invention
- Arrangement
- Style

- Memory
- Delivery

This is the traditional framework for public speaking and persuasive communication ancient Greek and Roman rhetoricians originally established. These canons provide a methodical approach to planning and delivering good speeches.

This was what the students were being taught, and they were given time during our sessions to compose their speech. They were seated in a college seminar classroom to write, much like a writing support group. "First and foremost, you must draft your speech," I told them. "Don't worry about developing your speaking style; it will come with time." As I continued to break down my structure as a speaker, I explained how a great speaker can tap into their audience's emotions and, like all great Marvel movies, you must start with a good introduction.

"Mr. De Nose, could I start with a joke?" a student asked.

With excitement, I exclaimed, "Absolutely! You might begin with humor or a quotation. There is no incorrect way to begin, but it is critical your introduction gets the attention of the audience, establishes rapport, and sets the tone for the rest of your speech. You need to hook the audience: start with a great opener that draws the audience's attention. A pertinent anecdote, a surprise fact or statistic, a thought-provoking question, a striking quotation, or a riveting tale can all be used. The idea is to catch the audience's interest and make them want to know more."

I told them they must clearly provide the relevance and value of their issue to the audience. "Explain why people should be interested in the topic and how it pertains to their lives, hobbies, or worries. This helps to establish a personal connection and demonstrates to the audience the worth of listening to your speech.

"The next vital step is to express the aim and thesis: Declare your speech's aim clearly and deliver a brief and focused thesis statement. This informs the audience and serves as a road map for your speech, and you must ensure your thesis statement is precise, detailed, and engaging, presenting the major argument or core point."

I informed them that they must present an overview by giving the audience a quick review of the important themes or elements of their speech. This assisted them in cognitively organizing the content as well as understanding the framework of their presentation. I advised them to keep it brief and to avoid delving into too much information.

The students were fully engaged, as if I was the one giving a speech.

Credibility was another important aspect. "Introduce yourself and briefly demonstrate your authority or subject-matter knowledge. Share any relevant experience, accomplishments, or certifications that support your knowledge and authority. This promotes trust and strengthens your oratorical credibility."

"But Mr. De Nose, what if we don't have any credibility?" one of my students asked.

I said, "Credibility is not solely determined by age or educational level but also by a combination of factors, including knowledge, expertise, character, and the ability to effectively communicate and support your ideas and claims."

Finally, I instructed them to establish the tone. "If your speech is going to be serious, inspiring, hilarious, or motivating, think about the tone you want to set for it and reflect that in your beginning. This promotes the right mood and an emotional connection with the audience.

"Remember to keep your introduction concise, focused, and engaging. Avoid going into too much detail or overwhelming the audience with information at this stage. The goal is to grab their attention, establish a connection, and create anticipation for the rest of your speech."

The students' eyes were filled with pride as they learned seeming to have a great sense of how to create a masterpiece of a speech.

They had the chance to read their speech to their senior peers in the following session, and I provided feedback on their stage presence, delivery, and style. I had them copy my actions, and I also offered them the option to critique one another. I encouraged the junior program participants to attend the seniors' speech during our final session. I also extended an invitation to other experts to visit and offer comments on their speeches. Juniors were merely there to observe so they could experience what next year looked like for them.

GREAT ORATORS

The importance of learning public speaking early on is a valuable investment in personal development. It equips individuals with essential skills that extend beyond the immediate context of public speaking, impacting academic success, professional growth, and overall communication effectiveness.

Studies have shown a fear of public speaking "inhibits promotion to management by 15 percent" and "cuts wages by 10 percent." It can also cost valuable sales for those who are self-employed according to the "Killer Pitch Master," Precious L. Williams.[1]

A successful job requires effective public speaking abilities. It gives you the capacity to speak clearly whether you are presiding over meetings, making suggestions, or making sales presentations. Your capacity to collaborate, negotiate, and persuade others—all of which are essential in professional settings—will be enhanced by having great communication skills.

It is essential for a fulfilling job since it increases your capacity for leadership, develops credibility, broadens your network, instills confidence, and gives you the ability to express ideas and affect change. Strong public speaking abilities may provide you an advantage in the workplace and lead to a wide range of chances.

Isshne, a former alumnus of my nonprofit who used to quake while she spoke during her speeches, stated, "Before I joined Leaders of the 21st Century, I was not so confident in speaking up, and I didn't like participating in any class discussions or group activities because those involved speaking up. However, this program has taught me many leadership skills and boosted my confidence in public speaking."

I have been surrounded by outstanding speakers from childhood to college. These speakers all had their own process of delivering a speech. They always applied the five canons of rhetoric. I did not know this then, but as I continued the path of a speaker and expanded my knowledge on teaching students how to give a speech, I realized I was exposed by four teachers who still serve as my mentors.

My father, pastor Rosmond De Nose, is the first great speaker I strongly appreciated. As a youngster, I used to observe my father writing his sermon for the upcoming Sunday while seated at the dining room table with different editions of the Bible and a piece of paper. Amazingly, I noticed less paper and more of his teachings being memorized as he and I grew older. Although he would occasionally utilize his Bible as a point of reference, the whole sermon was delivered from memory. I always liked the introduction.

He would guide you on a trip utilizing hermeneutics and exegesis. He motivated and inspired others. He was analytical and explanatory. He was thoughtful and contemplative, making sure to leave us with useful advice. As he delivered his sermon to the assembly, you could sense the empathy and compassion in his voice. I had never encountered a superb orator before. I had no idea seeing him every Sunday would make me a better public speaker. His strategy was to encourage spiritual development and a closer relationship with faith.

President of Hobart and Williams Smith Colleges, Mark Gearan, was the next outstanding speaker to whom I had the pleasure of being introduced through mentorship. His speaking style tended to be collaborative and personable with the goal of establishing a connection with professors, staff, students, and the larger academic community. He was a tactful visionary who spoke in a way that inspired others. He participated in ceremonial occasions as well as advocacy and fundraising activities. I made notes about how succinct he was in each speech he gave. He would modify his speaking techniques to fit various audiences and situations, keeping the context and goal of his speech in mind. You could hear how he achieved consensus and maintained a laser-like concentration on the mission and values of the colleges as he delivered his speech.

Senator Cory Booker was the next person from whom I learned how to produce a fantastic speech after I graduated from college. Renowned for his passionate and dynamic speaking manner, he added anecdotes and personal experiences into his remarks. He could tell a good tale. Booker conveyed material with high-energy movements, expressive facial animation, and verbal emphasis. He incited enthusiasm because he was impassioned. As a fervent supporter of justice and social equality, Booker's speeches frequently focused on these issues, as well as on hope and a general sense of optimism for the future. His conversational tone and background ranged from being mayor to senator.

Eric Stevenson, my employer as a community organizer, was my final exposure mentor to superb public speaking.

As a nonprofit executive with a range of speaking styles, I was always intrigued with his word choice. He was a Harvard graduate who could successfully communicate complicated thoughts and theories while delivering facts in a straightforward and succinct manner. In his speaking engagements, he contributed his own personalities, experiences, religion, and his Chicago flair. He addressed his speaking appearances with a deliberate and analytical perspective, as well as a goal-oriented strategy.

During my time with these men, each gave me the opportunity to learn from and observe them. They molded me into a better leader and human being. Now that I am a husband and parent, I find myself using my dining room table as a platform to motivate my son and daughters to exceed their own standards in all they do.

This was another aspect in my own life where exposure to mentors shaped my views and approach to public speaking. As I reflected more on it, I decided to reach out to Tim Wills to get his perspective on exposure mentorship.

Tim at one point was a stranger to me. Even though he spoke on stage at a conference in front of thousands of people, it often seemed as if he was speaking to me. His ability to convey a message on the importance of mentorship was solely done effectively because of his communication skills. He reached a level of success early in his career and has been on a path of reshaping mentorship programs in the United States by speaking to thousands of people annually. The pendulum swung toward an increase in mentors and exposure for mentees due to Tim's eloquent speaking ability.

How did he get to where he is today? His speech captivated me and inspired me to learn more of who he is.

I questioned Tim Wills during our discussion. "Can exposure mentorship shape the DEI pipeline for companies and organizations?"

Tim didn't hesitate to answer. "You know, in leadership, 99 percent of it is just showing up, and the other 1 percent is bringing people along with you in that process."

I nodded as Tim continued, and I reflected on my own leadership experiences. "So, I think one of the most important things for mentors to do—especially young people of color—is to expose them to their day to day lives."

I had always felt this way, but hearing it from someone who had spent most of his life in mentoring positions was encouraging. Tim was the youngest CEO of Boys & Girls Club of America in the country, at twenty-eight years old. He oversaw a large organization with over four thousand young people and led a large team.

Tim continued. "So if you're going to a fancy dinner party, take a young person with you who won't ever have that experience because we know that in life it's not about what you know, it's not about how many degrees you have or any of that stuff. It's really about the web of supporters you have and the network you have that propels you forward."

Tim was correct, and as I looked at him, I noticed a parallel between our lives because we both had the appropriate individuals cross our paths and the willingness to step out on a limb and extend ourselves to become better version of ourselves.

"And so I just urge folks that whenever possible, as a mentor, the best way to expose young people to the wonders of mentoring is to bring them along with your own experiences so they build a network, and see how they create their own web of supporters," Tim said. I felt the sincerity in his voice.

Tim's comments have stayed with me, and when Isshne spoke and I heard the assurance in her voice, I knew we had followed his advice correctly. We provided Isshne, born in Sri Lanka and immigrated to United States as a young child, the opportunity to amplify her voice. In the fall of 2023, she enrolled at Montclair State University and declared a major in earth and environmental science.

FINAL LESSONS

Becoming a great speaker in your chosen field can bring several benefits and opportunities. While professionalism may require dedication, continuous learning, and adherence to high standards, the rewards and opportunities it can bring make the journey worthwhile.

Aiming to become a professional with public speaking skills can result in job development, personal fulfillment, and the chance to have a significant impact in your field of choice. Speaking in front of an audience becomes essential as your leadership and professional career develop. You will have an advantage to get into rooms and onto platforms that many others do not have if you get the chance to study other outstanding speakers or shadow successful speakers.

Just as you would follow a sports team or your favorite musician, find speakers you admire as a role model. Emulate some of their best qualities, but remember to find your own style and voice.

Effective communication is a key skill in the workplace, and mastering the art of public speaking can significantly enhance your career and personal development. Great speakers exhibit strong leadership qualities. The ability to communicate a vision, inspire others, and influence decisions is crucial for leadership positions in organizations. You can articulate ideas and instructions clearly, fostering better collaboration within teams. This skill is particularly important in project management and team-based work environments.

A mentor can help you with this important skill by creating speaking opportunities for you and teaching you how to engage in conversations. They can have a profound impact on your professional success. Not only can they boost your communication skills, but they can enhance your leadership and networking capabilities, positioning yourself as an asset in your workplace and industry.

Find your platform! Who will prepare the stage for you? What is your rhetoric?

CHAPTER 10

The Future of Exposure Mentorship: A Call to Act

What is the purpose of your life? I once heard someone say two important days in life are the day you were born and the day you discovered why you were born.

I founded the nonprofit Leaders of the 21st Century with the mission to develop civic-minded youth leaders in urban communities and to prepare them for the world of work and beyond. The objective is simple: create social justice young leaders, and prepare them for career opportunities.

Promising students are identified in partnership with local schools for our two-year fellowship program. Our students receive tailored leadership and career development workshops to enhance their opportunity to navigate life after transitioning from high school to the real world. The two-year curriculum is broken into twenty-four sessions and our students are empowered to address Newark's challenges through project-based learning.

As the executive director, I also facilitate the curriculum for our students. Portions of the program are highly structured learning and development sessions. Saturday workshops provide our student leaders a hands-on approach to civic leadership and career readiness. The professional development workshops include but are not limited to Networking 101, Branding Yourself, Public Speaking, Presentation Collaboration, and Interview Skills with Human Resources. The social justice development includes but is not limited to the workshops Power, Privilege Justice, Ethical Decision Making, The Moral Purpose of Leadership.

To support the focus on career readiness, leadership, professional skills development, and civic engagement, professionals assist in mentoring our students through exposure by visiting our Saturday program and presenting to them. By the end of completing our program, students have an additional twenty-four highly skilled professional adults within their network.

My hope is to cut the economic gap for people of color by providing them with the knowledge, connections, and mentorship for a more equitable, just, inclusive, and diverse world.

Although I founded the organization in 2016, I worked a full-time job working as an administrator. After work and on the weekends, I dedicated myself to create a curriculum and teach students on Saturdays how to lead effectively as social change agents, as well as how to prepare themselves for employment and internships. It was a juggling act with balancing my full-time job and sacrificing my weekends. Nevertheless, I felt I was called to do this.

After four years of leading the organization, I prayed and fasted, seeking direction for my next steps. On June 30, 2020, amid a world pandemic, I decided to not return to my job and committed all my efforts to fully develop the organization. I felt deep in my soul it was a disservice to not fully dedicate myself to the mission and development to better support our youth.

I did not receive a salary—only a stipend. I lived off my savings during that time. Despite this, I believed in all my heart that I was called to change the world and make our world a better place. The young people who participated in Leaders of the 21st Century received all the necessary tools to make a difference in their community and to become career ready. They were who I wished to be when I was their age—clear minded with a clear sense of purpose yet understanding the areas in which they lacked while being eager to improve them.

We all know the first job out of college can have serious impacts on the rest of our lives. I was extremely fortunate for the opportunities in mine. If only students were exposed to the knowledge provided within our curriculum prior to college or graduating from high school. How better off would they be? How much of an impact could we make in our community? Our local community would be better, as well as our world.

Just as I received access to the many opportunities, I wish to do the same.

"Dan, I love what you are doing with our youth and would love to figure out how to bring you into our building," my high school Principal G said. "But we are limited on funding to bring in your program."

"I understand," I said with disappointment.

One of our programs called Leaders of the 21st Century Fellowship allows students to attend our Saturday sessions, which simulates applying for college. It is designed to give the students the experience to prepare them for the college application process. They must provide two letters of recommendations, write a personal statement, provide their transcript, and complete the application. Also, they must have a minimum of a 2.5 GPA. However, most of the students who apply average a 3.8 GPA. These students are typically aware of their next steps toward post-secondary options, but many of them lack soft skills, career readiness, public speaking, and exposure of professions and leadership development.

The curriculum provided to the seniors in our Saturday program is also the designated lesson plan for students within the school day. Rather than the students being part of the Saturday fellowship, we provided a workshop series called Powerskills: College, Career, and Beyond.

My disappointment was not so much about the principal not having the Powerskills program in the school building during the day. It was more that the students who typically do not apply for a developmental program such as ours will no longer be reached.

"Principal G, please let me know if we can work with your students in other ways," I said. "If you want me to come in as a speaker, I can do that as well."

Unfortunately, "no other options at the moment" was his response.

The frustration continued as we entered the new year of recruiting students to participate in the fellowship. We received the largest number of applications but due to lack of funding, could only take twenty-five students per cohort.

I was let down by the fact that a group of only fifty students would receive this information once a year. I asked myself, "Am I making a difference? Is this worth continuing?" I contemplated next steps. Funding is not where I need it to be to serve more students, and after three years of doing this full time, I still do not have a salary.

As a father of three and a husband, I was torn as if the earth was beginning to split underneath my feet. I needed to decide what my next steps would be. With my daughter entering college in the next year, student loans from undergraduate school, mortgage, bills, and all the other financial responsibilities, I knew my time was coming to an end although my wife continued to support me.

My professor would always say during my grant writing class, "No money, no mission." How can the mission continue without the funding? How can the mission continue of LOT21C if I am not able to provide for myself or family"

There is still hope...

I sat in my car overwhelmed, distraught for a while, before my cell phone rang.

"Hi, Mr. De Nose. How are you? This is Jeremiah."

When I first met Jeremiah for his Leaders of the 21st Century interview, I was immediately struck by how radiant he is. Later, he approached me before our first session on the New Jersey Institute of Technology college campus, saying, "Mr. De Nose, I am so thankful to be a part of this program! Last year, I lost my father, and he was someone I was very close to."

When I heard this, I felt a special obligation to him and to the other students, and it reminded me of a student named Doussou who graduated from our program two years earlier. She was able to obtain her associate degree while in high school and currently attends Emory University to study medicine. In her last year leading up to graduation from LOT21C, she lost one of her parents too.

"Hey, Jeremiah. I'm doing well. Just hanging in there." I did not want to share with him how I was truly feeling in the moment. "What's going on? Is everything okay?" I asked to try to take my thoughts off the earlier conversation and the multiple thoughts bouncing around like a pinball machine. I wanted to make sure he was all right.

"Everything is fine. I wanted to let you know that I got accepted into Harvard on a full ride."

Tears began to flow down my cheeks. "Congratulations. I am so proud of you!"

The students entering the program have unique stories, but this was the first time I became emotional.

After I congratulated Jeremiah, he said, "I wouldn't have gotten in if it wasn't for Leaders of the 21st Century."

"I appreciate that, but we are only a small piece of your story, and so many people on your path helped get you here."

"Yes, this is true, but what you have taught me gave me confidence and a network that has helped me," he said.

During our graduation ceremony for our students in the program, Jeremiah had this to say: "LOT21C enabled me to access platforms I never thought I would be able to speak publicly on and to take advantage of opportunities for advocacy that have continuously come in waves because of this organization and its efforts toward developing youth leaders in urban centers like Newark—young people like me who walk in their first session not thinking they would be able to go to college to being admitted into three Ivy League schools."

I posted a picture of him, his college acceptance, and a quote from his graduation speech. Many people throughout our community joined in to celebrate him.

"Dan, I have a number of my mentees, six, at Harvard now. Please let me know how I can help and connect him with them, so he has a support team of Black men when he arrives." It's all about building their networks.

In 2023, Jeremiah entered his first year at Harvard with a network, a brand, public speaking skills, an understanding of how to code-switch genuinely, a team of mentors, and also the knowledge of how to identify and build his board of mentors when entering college. He is an example of what exposure mentorship looks like when done correctly.

The news of Jeremiah gave me a boost to keep the flame of motivation burning. I knew how special of a program we created and how far our students have come in terms of development. Knowing this and believing this still did not solve my problem of funding and providing our program to students during their school day.

A few months after the great news I received a phone call.

"Dan, I really love the work you are doing and would like to bring you on board as a partner organization," Leena said. Her timing was not happenstance. It was divine intervention.

Leena serves as the executive director of a larger nonprofit that places organizations in career technical education classes during the school day. LOT21C is currently supporting more than 350 students across six high schools as part of her student ecosystem of support.

Serving more pupils was a major victory. We are proud of the work we have done and are currently helping students with their post-secondary transitions after graduating from high school. However, thousands of communities still need us.

Our efforts are still constrained—not because we lack motivation, but rather because of grants and other financial contributions.

When I asked Mr. Gerry if he could point me in the right direction on grant opportunities, I did not know what to expect.

Mr. Gerry and his entire family are the benefactors to Lake Delaware Boys Camp—the summer program I mentioned in the earlier chapter. He is the descendant of one of America's founding fathers, Elbridge Gerry, who served as the fifth vice president of the United States under James Madison.

He agreed to take me under his wing and mentor me on a grant proposal with a large foundation. Here is another example of the power of exposure. After each draft, he would give me feedback and provide edits to my proposal. We spoke over the phone after each revised version.

Out of all my years, this was the first time someone gave me this type of mentoring in developing a grant.

After the third revision, the grant proposal was all set to be submitted.

It was during a Saturday session when I noticed a missed call. *That's odd*, I thought, knowing that on a Saturday, aside from my family, I don't get phone calls. My phone notifications dinged, and a text asked to call back.

When I looked closely to who the sender of the text was, it was from the chairman of the foundation for the grant I applied to. I knew I would not be able to call back until after the LOT21C class ended, so I did my best to compartmentalize the present moment of teaching class and the possibility of not receiving good news.

"Okay, everyone. Have a great rest of the weekend!" I bellowed as I shepherded my students to the classroom exit.

Without thinking twice, I scurried across the empty classroom of the NJIT campus and sat at a desk. Dialing his number was like a child unwrapping a gift but not knowing what was inside the box. I felt a sense of excitement mixed with nervousness. I did not know what to expect but prepared myself for the worst.

"Dan, I have some good news and some bad news," the board chair said after a few pleasant salutations to one another. "The bad news is we did not approve you for the amount you asked for."

My head pressed against my left hand to catch my head as it dropped. I took a deep breath to gain composure.

"The good news is we decided to approve you for more than you asked for. We believe in the work you are doing, and we believe in you. We need more programs like yours, and our education system is doing a disservice in not teaching our young people what you are teaching."

I wept.

"Thank you so much for funding my organization," I said as I wiped my tears away with the corner of my long sleeve.

The grant allocation was given in the year 2023 as a three-year matching grant that was to be dispersed in thirds. To receive a third of the grant, I must raise the same amount. The work now continues as this was the largest grant LOT21C has ever received.

I believe the program we offer during the week and on the weekends can be implemented in all of the country's school districts. To make this feasible, there are three essential components. It is necessary to form partnerships with a school board, a college or university, and a sizable corporation. These three groups are the ideal trifecta.

THE FUTURE OF EXPOSURE MENTORSHIP

EXPOSURE OPPORTUNITIES

We can replicate Jeremiah's success as well as all of the other students who participate in Leaders of the 21st Century fellowship. Students of color who come from urban communities such as Newark are being prepared to enter the workforce and gain the experience needed to be successful in their career. Having exposure to opportunities through mentors gives an advantage and provides chances of being guided, supported, and mentored by experienced individuals in a given field or industry. Exposure mentorship typically takes seasoned professionals who provide guidance, advice, and expertise based on their own knowledge and experiences and brings students into their world of work.

Exposure to opportunities through mentors can be beneficial by granting them access to networks. Through their guidance, students may gain access to new networks, professional associations, and contacts that can open doors to job opportunities, collaborations, and introductions to influential individuals.

Mentors can also provide valuable insights and insider knowledge about the industry or field. They can share their experiences, best practices, and lessons learned, helping students navigate challenges, avoid common pitfalls, and understand the unwritten rules of the profession. This insider knowledge can be crucial for identifying and seizing opportunities.

In Jeremiah's case, his network from LOT21C provided him a letter of recommendation. His letter came from the vice president of the largest school board in New Jersey.

Skills development and learning from mentors can offer guidance and help mentees identify areas for improvement. The mentors can provide constructive feedback, suggest relevant training or resources, and offer advice on honing specific skills in demand within their industry. This skills development can enhance the mentee competitiveness and increase their chances of securing desirable opportunities.

Mentors bring diverse perspectives and experiences to the table. They can broaden thinking, challenge assumptions, and expose mentees to alternative approaches or ways of looking at things. This exposure to different perspectives can spark creativity, help students think critically, and broaden their understanding of the field, potentially leading to innovative ideas and opportunities.

Mentors also can advocate for students and provide recommendations for job opportunities, connect them with influential individuals, or endorse their skills and capabilities. The mentor's support and endorsement can significantly increase the mentee's visibility and credibility, making it more likely for them to be considered for important opportunities.

Mentors can challenge you to set higher goals, push your boundaries, and support students in overcoming obstacles. Their mentorship can foster a student's self-confidence, resilience, and ambition, empowering them to seize opportunities and reach their full potential.

FUTURE OF COLLEGES

The future where we provide opportunities for students of color reminds me of the interview with Kim in an earlier chapter, who asked a great question: "What are chancellors doing about the curriculum of the future?" She believes colleges need to head in the direction to get students ready for the workforce. Students cannot transition into the workplace because they do not have the life skills to go along with it.

The growing concern is this: what are the benefits of getting into major debt and not having a job to pay off the debt after college, especially with the rising cost of a college education?

Many colleges and universities are working toward finding ways to mitigate the rising costs and provide more accessible education through scholarships, grants, and financial aid programs, but this is not enough. Partnerships between colleges and the workforce are extremely important to bridge the gap between education and employment. Such collaborations aim to align the skills and knowledge imparted in college programs with the needs and demands of the workforce.

The solution is to collaborate with employers and industry professionals, where colleges can develop curricula that are more responsive to the evolving needs of the job market. This ensures students acquire the knowledge and skills in demand, increasing their employability upon graduation. Work-based learning opportunities, such as internships, co-op programs, and apprenticeships, allow students to apply their classroom learning in real-world settings, gain practical skills, and develop professional networks.

Colleges must bring industry experts into the educational process, allowing colleges to tap into their knowledge and insights. This helps colleges stay updated on industry trends, technological advancements, and emerging skill requirements, enabling them to adjust their programs accordingly. There should be collaboration with the workforce that improves job placement rates for graduates. Employers can provide input on the skills they seek in candidates, participate in career fairs, and offer mentoring or networking opportunities, all of which contribute to better employment prospects for students.

During a career expo event, a panelist who did not attend an Ivy League school mentioned most of the human resources department would only recruit from Ivy Leagues, missing out on a slew of great candidates. The workforce would need to diversify their outreach to colleges that do not fit their traditional recruitment process.

Workforce partnerships can extend beyond initial education and support lifelong learning. Colleges can collaborate with employers to offer professional development programs, upskilling initiatives, and continuing education courses that cater to the needs of working professionals, enabling them to stay relevant in their careers.

PARTNERSHIPS BETWEEN HIGH SCHOOL AND THE WORKFORCE

Partnerships between high schools and the workforce are valuable in preparing students for future careers and facilitating a smooth transition from education to the professional world. Career exploration and guidance by collaborating with the workforce allows high schools to provide students with exposure to various industries and careers. Through partnerships with employers, students can participate in career fairs, job shadowing, mentorship programs, and internships, giving them firsthand experience and insight into different career pathways.

School districts provide professional development for educators, so collaboration with the workforce provides opportunities for professional development for high school educators. They can gain insights into industry trends, emerging technologies, and evolving job requirements, which help them enhance their instructional practices and better prepare students for the workforce. School districts can redesign their curriculum to be more industry informed.

If done right, engaging with employers and industry experts could allow school districts to design curricula and learning experiences that reflect current industry standards and practices. This ensures students are equipped with the skills and knowledge sought by employers, enhancing their employability after graduation.

Every school has school counselors. There should be an enhanced career counseling and job placement departments that allow workforce partnerships to enhance career counseling services in high schools. Employers can contribute to career guidance sessions, provide information about job opportunities, and participate in mock interviews. This support helps students make informed decisions about their career paths and improves their chances of successful job placement.

Lastly, collaborating with the workforce would allow high schools to identify gaps in the local job market. By understanding the needs of employers, schools can develop targeted programs to bridge these gaps, ensuring students possess the skills required for in-demand careers.

The sooner students are exposed to this information and receive guidance through exposure mentorship, the quicker we should see significant differences in our community as well as the pipeline to support diversity, equity, and inclusion.

FINAL LESSONS: CALL TO ACTION — THE MENTORSHIP MANIFESTO

As we conclude this transformative journey through the chapters of *The Power of Exposure: Lessons of Success from Highly Effective Mentors*, it becomes evident that rejection is not a roadblock but a catalyst for growth. From conquering self-doubt to fostering strategic alliances and promoting diversity, equity, and inclusion, each chapter reiterates the profound impact of mentorship. This book has unfolded the lessons of success derived from highly effective mentors.

Now, as you close this book, I invite you to take inspired action:

1. Embrace your journey: Recognize failures and rejections may be strong drivers of personal and professional growth. Accept your unique journey, knowing each rejection has the ability to change things for the better.
2. Conquer self-doubt with mentorship: Recognize the value of mentorship in overcoming imposter syndrome. Seek for mentors who can guide, encourage, and help you navigate challenges with confidence.
3. Build meaningful relationships: Cultivate small moments with big impact. Foster genuine mentor-mentee connections, understanding that even the smallest interactions can lead to significant transformations.

4. Strategic alliances for impact: Understand the strategic power of alliances in mentorship. Create networks that amplify your impact and contribute to your professional and personal growth.

5. Champion diversity, equity, and inclusion: Commit to making mentorship a great equalizer. Foster diversity in mentorship relationships, creating an inclusive environment that allows everyone to thrive.

6. Cultivate transformative connections: Recognize the power of mentorship and networking in transforming lives. Actively seek opportunities to connect with mentors and fellow professionals to foster a community that propels everyone forward.

7. Navigate spaces authentically: Trust in your brilliance and navigate professional spaces with authenticity. Let mentorship guide you in showcasing your true self and realizing your potential.

8. Master code-switching for growth: Learn the language of success through code-switching. Master the art of adapting to different professional environments, using mentorship as a tool to refine your communication skills.

9. Leverage mentorship in public speaking: Explore the uncharted territory beyond the podium. Harness the power of mentorship in public speaking, refining your skills and making a lasting impact through effective communication.

10. Answer the call to act: The future of exposure mentorship lies in your hands. Answer the call to act by becoming a mentor, seeking mentorship, and actively participating in mentorship programs. Contribute to a future where mentorship is a cornerstone of personal and professional development.

Remember, the story doesn't end here. Your journey is a testament to the transformative power of exposure mentorship. Take this call to act seriously because in shaping your future, you also contribute to shaping the futures of others.

Ignite your potential, champion mentorship, serve as a sponsor, and let the ripple effect of your actions create a world where transformative exposure mentorship becomes the precursor to unprecedented success. The future of exposure mentorship is one decision away, and this manifesto starts with you.

Acknowledgments

I would like to extend my heartfelt gratitude to those who supported and believed in this project from its inception. Your early commitment and enthusiasm have been a source of inspiration throughout the writing process. Thank you for being the first champions of this work; your belief in my words has added immeasurable value to the journey of bringing this book to life.

DIAMOND

Mark Gearan

Jadil Jimenez

Mary O' Malley

PLATINUM

Rosmond and Marcely De Nose

Harry Pozycki

Jim and Wendra Trowbridge

GOLD

Richard Burdett

Modia Butler

SILVER

Tricia Brewster

Devonne De Nose

Juail Goode

David Grome

Nia Jervier

Everett Johnson

Rick Keshishian

Katie Peglow

Khaatim Sherrer El

Thomas Spencer

Marlene Thomas-Inman

BRONZE

Ronald Andrews

Luke Apicella

Paul Ashburn

Jeffery Asiedu

Innis Baah

Tanya Barrow

LaToya Battle-Brown

Lisa Bento

Timothy and Margaret Bergeron

Mary Bergeron

Vanessa Blake

Allan Boomer

Thomas Bozzuto

Frank Carey
Fawn Cater
Tracy Cherry
Tia Collier
Leslie & Mark Comesañas
Tasha L. Cooper
Pamela B. Daniels
Shari Dann
Barbara De Nose
Karen De Nose
Erline De Nose
Deidre Farmbry
Helena Fish
Andrew Fosbrook
Isaias Garcia
Cliff Gardner
Nate Georges
Trevor Gionet
Stephen Green
Kwaku Gyasi
Jack Harris
Ketlyn Henry
Chris Jenco
Yadiria Jimenez
Eric Koester
Traymanesha Lamy
Margaret Landi

Kwame Lovell
Vernessa Mason-Mitchell
Dr. Janelle McIntosh-Evans
Jonathan Molloy

Janher Morisset
Tiffany Murphy
Victor Nelson
Susan Pliner
Zara Pyle
Adam Ravener
Victoria Ravener
Marc Saint-Louis
Colleen Sinclair
John Standish
Heidi Swain
Jennie Sylne
Nasha Thomas
Jean Trujillo
Jomal Vailes
Sheila Venable
Sandy Wagner
Tiffany Walker
Cathy Williams
Lavar Young
Maureen Zupan

D.M. DE NOSE SUPPORTERS
Nikki Anderson
Shamire Archibald
Carol Bergeron
Andrew Binger
Shirley Blaise
Alfred Blake
Chantal Borgella
Sarah Brillant
Jason Bryant

Alexander Cena
John Cromartie
LaTrace Dabney
Myisha De Nose
Lorna Demosthenes
AnnMarie Drummond
Ronald Fazio
Katie Flowers
Emma Flowers
Devin Gabriel
Theresa Gage
Deaka Goldson
Tameka Green-Foote
Ryan Hemnarine
Carrie Hessney
Nicholas Howie
Lisa Inman
Patty Jessie
Phil Kent
Barbara Martinez
Sherrice Massiah
Annie McManus
Laura Metellus
Ihsaan Muhammad
Caroline Murphy
Rosetta Nairne
Dannie Napoleon
Caitlin O'Brien
Kathy Overbeke
Matthew Ozoria
Charisse Palmer
Cynthia Pierre-Louis

Steven Pierre-Paul
Loha Raphael
Matt Reiners
Nicole Rennie
Sabrina Rose
Ava Shapiro
Carolyn Sharaway
Regina Sharpe
John Simon
Erin Sweeney
Roberson Sylne
Tonnica Thomas
Deidre Thompson
Michelina Thornton
Marisol Torres
Nate Trowbridge
Fabian Velez
April Venable
Sean Warner
Kenitra Washington
Richard Wasserman
Dale Watkins
Khalilah Webster

Appendix

INTRODUCTION

1. Benjamin Harris and Sydney Schreiner Wertz, "Racial Differences in Economic Security: The Racial Wealth Gap. US Department of The Treasury," US Department of Treasury, News, last modified September 15, 2022, https://home.treasury.gov/news/featured-stories/racial-differences-economic-security-racial-wealth-gap.

2. "Wealth distribution in the United States in the third quarter of 2023," Statista, Statistics, last modified December 20, 2023, https://www.statista.com/statistics/203961/wealth-distribution-for-the-us/.

3. National Center for Education Statistics, *Condition of Education*, "College Enrollment Rates" (Institute of Education Sciences: US Department of Education, 2023), https://nces.ed.gov/programs/coe/indicator/cpb/college-enrollment-rate.

4. "Unemployment in December 2010," US Bureau of Labor Statistics, Publications, The Economics Daily, last modified January 11, 2011, https://www.bls.gov/opub/ted/2011/ted_20110111.htm.

CHAPTER 1

1. Meilan Solly, "The True Story Behind the Harriet Tubman Movie," *Smithsonian Magazine*, October 30, 2019, https://www. smithsonianmag.com/smithsonian-institution/true-story-harriet-tubman-movie-180973413/.

2. Les Brown, "Les Brown: You Gotta Be Hungry (Full Transcript)," The Singju Post, September 2, 2016, transcript by Pangambam S, https://singjupost.com/les-brown-you-gotta-be-hungry-full-transcript/.

3. "Hobart and William Smith Colleges," US News & World Report, last modified 2022, https://www.usnews.com/best-colleges/hobart-and-william-2731.

4. John F. Kennedy, "Ask Not What Your Country Can Do For You," US History, Historic Documents, transcription by Independence Hall Association, January 20, 1961, https://www. ushistory.org/documents/ask-not.htm.

CHAPTER 2

1. Tim Russert, *Big Russ and Me: Father and Son: Lessons of Life* (New York; Hachette Books, 2014).

2. Ibid.

3. Julia Link Roberts, "Parents Can be Mentors, Too!" *Gifted Child Today* 15, no.3 (May/June 1992), https://doi. org/10.1177/107621759201500310.

CHAPTER 3

1. Evan Casey, "How Can Code-Switching Be Used as a Positive? This Wauwatosa Professor Wrote a Book about It," *Milwaukee Journal Sentinel*, June 3, 2022, https://www.jsonline.com/story/communities/west/news/wauwatosa/2022/01/03/wauwatosa-professor-george-paasewe-writes-book-code-switching/8799472002/.

CHAPTER 5

1. Mentor National, *The Mentoring Effect* (Boston, MA: Mentor National, 2024), https://www.mentoring.org/resource/the-mentoring-effect/.

2. "Why do we perform better when someone has high expectations of us?" The Decision Lab, Biases, last modified 2024, https://thedecisionlab.com/biases/the-pygmalion-effect.

3. "Business Psychology: Golem Effect vs. Pygmalion Effect," Brescia University, Management News, last modified December 14, 2017, https://www.brescia.edu/2017/12/golem-effect-vs-pygmalion-effect/.

4. CHAPTER 6

1. Martha Irvine, "When Teen Pregnancy Runs in the Family," *Los Angeles Times*, December 8, 2002, https://www.latimes.com/archives/la-xpm-2002-dec-08-adna-ties8-story.html

2. Collen O'Dea, "Census Shows NJ Had Highest Median Household Income of Any State in 2022," *NJ Spotlight News*, September 18, 2023, https://www.njspotlightnews.org/2023/09/asian-black-hispanic-median-household-income-2022-seniors-child-poverty-poverty-rate-official-poverty-limit/.

CHAPTER 7

1. "What is Networking, and Why Do You Need to Do It?" Columbia University Center for Career Education, Resources, 2024, March 11, 2024, https://www.careereducation.columbia.edu/resources/what-networking-and-why-do-you-need-do-it.

2. "CDF Freedom Schools," Children's Defense Fund, Our Work, n.d., accessed January 12, 2024, https://www.childrensdefense.org/programs/cdf-freedom-schools/.

3. "Our Mission," Untied Way, Our Impact, n.d., accessed January 27, 2024, https://www.unitedway.org/our-impact/mission.

4. "New ACE Report Presents Data on College Presidents Who Are Black," *The Journal of Blacks in Higher Education*, April 24, 2023, https://jbhe.com/2023/04/new-ace-report-presents-data-on-college-presidents-who-are-black/.

CHAPTER 8

1. "What is Code-Switching," dictionary.com, June 18, 2018, https://www.dictionary.com/e/code-switching/.

CHAPTER 9

1. Precious Williams, "5 Doors That Public Speaking Skills Can Open in Your Career," *Pulse* (blog), LinkedIn, September 13, 2020, https://www.linkedin.com/pulse/5-doors-public-speaking-skills-can-open-your-career/.

www.ingramcontent.com/pod-product-compliance
Lightning Source LLC
Chambersburg PA
CBHW070859160726
48004CB00003B/1152